Christ, Our Compass
Making Moral Choices

Alfred McBride, O.Praem.

RESCRIPT
In accord with the Code of Canon Law, I hereby grant my permission to publish *Christ Our Compass: Making Moral Choices*, by Alfred McBride, O.PRAEM.
Most Reverend Joseph R. Binzer
Auxiliary Bishop
Vicar General
Archdiocese of Cincinnati
Cincinnati, Ohio
December 3, 2013
The Imprimatur ("Permission to Publish") is a declaration that a book or pamphlet is considered to be free from doctrinal or moral error. It is not implied that those who have granted the *Imprimatur* agree with the contents, opinions or statements expressed.

Cover and book design by Mark Sullivan
Cover image © Irina Tischenko | PhotoXpress

LIBRARY OF CONGRESS CATALOGING-IN-PUBLICATION DATA
McBride, Alfred.
Christ, our compass : making moral choices / Alfred McBride, O.PRAEM.
pages cm
Includes bibliographical references and index.
ISBN 978-1-61636-711-4 (alk. paper)
1. Christian ethics—Catholic authors. I. Title.
BJ1249.M145 2013
241'.042—dc23
2013041398

ISBN 978-1-61636-711-4

Published by Franciscan Media
28 W. Liberty St.
Cincinnati, OH 45202
www.FranciscanMedia.org

Printed in the United States of America.
Printed on acid-free paper.
14 15 16 17 18 5 4 3 2 1

CONTENTS

INTRODUCTION

When people speak ill of you, so live that nobody will believe them.

—Plato, *The Republic*

THROUGHOUT THIS BOOK, WE WILL examine moral living through the lens of "Life in Christ," the third part of the *Catechism of the Catholic Church*. There are two sections in "Life in Christ." Section One considers the basics of the moral life, such as Christ's laws of love, the role of God's grace, the reality of sin and its forgiveness, and the power of happiness as a motive for Christian living. That section is the foundation for Section Two, which explores the meaning of the Ten Commandments and the path to holiness they describe.

Following the pattern in the two sections of "Life in Christ," *Christ, Our Compass* will devote four chapters to the basics of Christian living and eight to the application of the Ten Commandments to our daily lives. Each chapter will highlight three things that the *Catechism* asks us to do.

In chapter one, I will show three ways in which the *Catechism*'s teaching on grace helps us be moral. First, the *Catechism* asks us to answer God's call to a love relationship. Second, we are asked to become who we are—a "new creation." Third, the *Catechism* asks us to let the joy of Jesus motivate us to be moral. The role of love and the fruit of joy compose the horizon of living the *Catechism*. Without a love relationship with Christ, we will have no passion in our faith life. Without a feeling of deep joy we will not understand the moral life.

The commandments describe goals of love that respond to the gracious gift of salvation from Jesus. They are more than legal rules. They are invitations from Christ to live our faith and to receive the powers of grace in the sacraments. There is yet a further step: living the *Catechism* by loving others graciously, generously, enthusiastically.

We all want happiness. Loving God and people, especially those in need, is a sure fire road to joy. The moral life is not meant to depress us; it is geared to authentic personal satisfaction.

Yet it may seem odd to add that such love of God and people includes the way of the cross. That is why we speak of sacrificial love. It is a myth to think the road of love contains no difficulties, problems, disappointments, or tragedies. Jesus, Son of God and son of Mary, loved us with all his heart, yet knew many trials. Living the part of the *Catechism* that deals with the moral life is grounded in these preliminary thoughts.

The structure of this book is composed of two parts. The first section describes the fundamental principles of our moral life. This is covered in our first three chapters. By beginning with God's grace and the joy of what true morality means, we have the highest possible means for the journey to goodness.

By then reflecting on the gift of the Church as our Mother and Teacher, we obtain the profound confidence we will need as we embark on the adventure of holiness. Jesus gave us the Church as a maternal source of his graces and wisdom. Jesus gave us the Church to discern the truths imparted to us in Scripture and Tradition, celebrated by us in the sacraments and enlightened by us in our prayer life.

By offering us a perfectly clear understanding of the reality of sin and evil, the *Catechism* lifts us out of a culture that prefers to counsel us to forget this truth. A failure to admit our sinfulness causes us to flee from reality, to misunderstand the purpose of Chris's salvation, and to be committed to a life shorn of true love and steady joy.

The second section of this book applies the principles just mentioned to practical ways we can live them everyday. In the nine chapters that follow, we develop the gifts of the moral life through guidance from the Ten Commandments. We base this interpretation on Christ's two greatest commandments as found in the Gospels.

"Teacher, which commandment in the law is the greatest?" He said to him, "'You shall love the Lord your God with all your heart, and with all your soul, and with all your mind.' This is the greatest and first commandment. And a second is like it: 'You shall love your neighbor as yourself.'" (Matthew 22:36–39)

Chapter four of this book calls us to love God as stated in commandments one and two. Chapter five asks us to reclaim the Sabbath, as we read in commandment three.

Chapters six through twelve emphasize the love of neighbor in family life, marriage, sexuality, war and peace, justice, commitment to truth, and the role of virtues in helping us to live these teachings. Of course the love of God and power of God's abundant spiritual graces remain an essential component of our coping with these challenges.

We also view the journey as our growth in holiness. We hear the call of our loving Father. We experience affection of Christ, who stands at the door of our hearts with the promise of walking with us. We are assured of the presence of the Holy Spirit, who gives us many gifts to be our light and the source of energy in our progress.

Generally each chapter contains a number of illustrations to make a point, and concludes with reflection questions to assist you on your path to God. It would be helpful, but not necessary, to have a copy of the *Catechism* handy as you read through this book.

I trust this text will invite you into God's presence and pray you will feel God's love for you increase in your faith journey.

CHAPTER ONE

Amazing Grace, What Joy It Brings!

C.S. Lewis is one of the most widely read religious writers in the English-speaking world. Born in Northern Ireland, he was taught to say his prayers and go to church, but he was not particularly interested in religion. He abandoned religion altogether during his student years at Oxford.

What drew him back to God? Lewis explained the experience in his book *Surprised by Joy*. It was a series of bursts of happiness that pulled him to God. He said a door to joy would open for a moment, then close again. It left him with an inner longing for "something or someone."

One night while he sat alone in his room at Magdalene College in Oxford, God lovingly took hold of him: "You must picture me alone in that room in Magdalene, feeling the steady, unrelenting approach of him whom I desired earnestly not to meet. In the Trinity term of 1929 I gave in, and admitted that God was God, and knelt and prayed: perhaps, that night, the most dejected and reluctant convert in all England." Moved by God's love and grace, Lewis became one of Christianity's most eloquent apologists.

His experience demonstrates the power of God's grace and the link between grace and happiness. There is no better departure point as we start this book on morality because living a moral life begins with God's grace and the promise of happiness.

Answer God's Call to Love

"Grace is *favor*, the *free and undeserved help* that God gives us to respond to his call to be children of God, partakers of the divine nature and eternal life" (*CCC*, 1996; emphasis in original).

Many people in our society see Christianity only as a set of rules: no abortions, restrictions on sexual freedom, no access to euthanasia—outsiders controlling our most intimate decisions. Others who fail to understand Christian morality also associate it only with rules. The starting point for Christian morality, however, is not rules or laws but God's gracious love for us and his appeal for love in return. Yes, there will and should be laws, but these flow from God's love for us and our desire to express our affection for him.

Responding to God's love is not always easy. The *Catechism* notes that St. Teresa of Avila understood the challenge: "Hope, O my soul, hope.... Dream that the more you struggle, the more you prove the love that you bear your God, and the more you will rejoice one day with your Beloved in a happiness and rapture that can never end" (*CCC*, 1821).

Living a moral life involves sacrificial love. When Pope John XXIII was patriarch of Venice, his photographer found him one morning at the bedside of his ailing secretary, Loris Capovilla. He had been there all night. The photographer said, "Eminence, you did not have to wear yourself out this way. Surely, the nuns would have looked after him." The future pope replied, "No, no, the sisters are very busy. They need their rest. Besides, I know exactly when to give him his medicine."

Mothers and fathers know this sacrificial love when they care for their sick children or work extra hours to make things better for their families. The beauty of all this is that Jesus loans us his love through grace. Unlike a credit card, though, there is never a spending limit. Our moral journey begins with a yes to Christ's call to a love relationship with him.

How do we know we have grace? The *Catechism* answers,

> Since it belongs to the supernatural order, grace escapes our experience and cannot be known except by faith. We cannot therefore rely on our feelings or our works to conclude that we are justified and saved.... Reflection on God's blessings in our life and in the lives of the saints offers us a guarantee that grace is at work in us and spurs us on to an ever greater faith and an attitude of trustful poverty. A pleasing illustration of this attitude is found in the reply of St. Joan of Arc to a question posed as a trap by her ecclesiastical judges: Asked if she knew that she was in God's grace, she replied: "If I am not, may it please God to put me in it; if I am, may it please God to keep me there." (*CCC*, 2005)

Become a New Creation

A turtle and a scorpion came to the bank of a river. The scorpion said, "I have an important appointment on the other side of the river. Please ferry me across." "No," said the turtle. "You will bite me on the neck, poison me, and we will drown." "I promise you I won't." "All right, climb aboard."

Midway across the river, the scorpion stung the turtle. Sadly, the turtle looked up at him. "You assured me you wouldn't do that." "I'm sorry," said the scorpion. "I didn't mean to. But I guess it's my nature." Jesus knew that if we were to become moral our natures needed transformation. Otherwise we would stay like the scorpion in the story.

As the *Catechism* says, "Grace is a *participation in the life of God*.... The grace of Christ is the gratuitous gift that God makes to us of his own life, infused by the Holy Spirit into our soul to heal it of sin and to sanctify it.... 'Therefore, if anyone is in Christ, he is a new creation' [2 Cor 5:17]" (*CCC*, 1997, 1999; emphasis in original).

We cannot overcome the weakness of our human nature on our own, but we can with God's grace. We have a higher possibility than the poor old scorpion. Consider three common approaches to the human condition: the pessimistic, the optimistic, and the realistic.

Pessimists say that humans are basically bad, so defend yourself against others. This idea was first expressed by the Roman playwright Titus Maccius Plautus, who, in his play *Asinaria* (195 B.C.), wrote, "*Lupus est homo homini*" ("Man is a wolf to his fellow man"). When Hitler rose to power in the 1930s the British Parliament refused to take action against him. Their pessimism scared them into fear of German power. Winston Churchill reminded them, "A pessimist sees the difficulty in every opportunity; an optimist sees the opportunity in every difficulty."

We will never see the rainbow by staring at the ground.

Pessimism is the denial of the possibilities of God's mighty power. Grace is stronger than sin. Love is stronger than death. In modern times, no greater example of this optimistic view was confirmed by the election of Pope John Paul II on October 16, 1978. At that time, the western world looked with fear and pessimism at the titanic military power of Russian Communism. Within a year, Pope John Paul II had flown to Warsaw, where he went to Victory Square to celebrate Mass for a million Polish people gathered to worship with him.

At the beginning of his homily the pope spoke of their desires. With joyful tears they chanted repeatedly, "We want God!" They sang the Latin hymn, "*Christus Vincit!*" Christ conquers. Christ reigns. Christ commands. A roar of hope and confidence in God arose that day from people with no army or guns or money. It was the beginning of the death knell of communism.

Realists claim we are indeed good at heart, but we are damaged. This was St. Augustine's view. We're not all bad and we're not all good. The Church embraces this view of human nature in her teaching on original sin. Because of the Fall of our first parents, we are born deprived of the graces and loving relationship with God that had once been theirs. We do not commit original sin, but we do inherit it (see CCC, 385–410).

Through the grace of baptism into the saving death and resurrection of Jesus, we are restored to a relationship with God and liberated from all sin, both original and actual. We become beautiful new people, filled with grace, goodness, and love. But unfortunately, the wounds of original sin remain. We are damaged. We find it hard to love. We easily let our passions take us over. We permit malice in our thoughts. We grow weary of searching for truth.

That is why we must resolve, in faith, to stay on the moral journey, empowered by the graces of prayer and the sacraments, especially reconciliation and the Eucharist. The experience is a collaboration between God and our freedom. "Indeed we also work, but we are only collaborating with God who works, for his mercy has gone before us. It has gone before us so that we may be healed, and follows us so that once healed, we may be given life" (*CCC*, 2001).

My second point, then, is this: Become who you are, a new creation in Jesus. Christian living will fulfill the potential locked in our baptism, the potential to be a new person at home, at work, and in society. It takes a lifetime, but is well worth the struggle.

In our new creation there is a new law, the law of love: "The New Law is called the *law of love* because it makes us act out of the love infused by the Holy Spirit, rather than from fear; a *law of grace*, because it confers the grace of strength to act by means of faith and the sacraments; a *law of freedom*, because it sets us free from the ritual observances of the Old Law and inclines us to act spontaneously by the prompting of charity." (*CCC*, 1972; emphasis in original).

Let Jesus's Joy Motivate You

Not long ago I asked a group of friends how I could convince people that happiness is a powerful motive for being moral. They all said that an invitation to faith in Jesus should be an essential part of my approach.

Christian morality works best in those who have a living, conscious, and active faith in Jesus Christ. As the *Catechism* says, "The Beatitudes respond to the natural desire for happiness. This desire is of divine origin. God has placed it in the human heart in order to draw man to the One who alone can fulfill it.... God alone satisfies" (*CCC*, 1718).

Conventional worldly wisdom complains that the Church's moral teachings make people miserable. But the Church argues that being moral is the only way to be happy. Augustine said it best: "In seeking you, my God, I seek a happy life" (*Confessions*, 10, 20). The prevalent despair, obsessive behavior, and anxiety in our culture arise not from being moral, but from the abandonment of the moral law in many cases. Those who think it's fun to be immoral are kidding themselves in the long run.

God wants us to be happy. "God put us in the world to know, to love, and to serve him, and so to come to paradise" (*CCC*, 1721). Jesus's greatest speech was the Sermon on the Mount, and his opening lines are all about how to be happy. That's what the eight beatitudes signify.

Having stated these principles of happiness, Jesus gave a series of rules that would make that possible. (For example, be reconciled with your brother, and then come and offer your gift at the altar.) And we already know he has given us the grace to absorb the principles of moral living and live his commandments.

Joy is a mark of sainthood. If you want happiness, we might say, make the right moral choices. I remember a book from some years ago, titled *Saints Are Not Sad*. In this book author Frank Sheed noted that people took too grim a view of saints, and he proceeded to show the genuine delight that has marked the lives of saints.

St. Philip Neri, for one, was living proof that the moral life need not be oppressive or depressing. He liked upsetting people's false expectations about saintliness. Philip's inner child found mischievous ways to achieve his goal, such as occasionally shaving only half of his beard, or dressing as a clown and walking the streets of Rome. Here was a happy man who loved God and loved people, and who resolved to do God's will.

The point here is not that bizarre behavior makes one happy, but that happiness is the goal of Christian life. Since we all want a joyful heart, why not live the good life that will make it happen?

Happiness is one of the most persuasive arguments for adopting Christian living. Just look at what happens when the opposite occurs. People addicted to drink, drugs, sex, and money have embarked on illusory paths to joy and been grabbed by forces stronger than they bargained for. The original buzz, rush, orgasm, or thrill may be fun or soothing. Yet whatever was attractive fades quickly as these behaviors make people their slaves and draw them into the black hole of misery. Thank God there are so many rescue groups, support communities, and dedicated people who offer their lives to bring the addicted and obsessed back to the possibilities of real joy.

How do we convince people that Christian living is the key to happiness? First, we should admit that our happiness is mixed with sorrow and the inevitable tragedies of life. There are no perfect families, perfect marriages, perfect parishes—nothing human is perfect. Part of our moral quest includes carrying our cross with Christ. I think that a sense of humor is the best way of revealing to others the Christian joy we experience.

Don't be afraid to struggle with doubt. Blaise Pascal appealed to the unbelievers of his day to consider the examples of others who struggled with their doubts and came to faith. "You want to come to faith, but you do not know the way," Pascal wrote. "Follow the way by which they set out: by acting as though they already believed."[1]

G.K. Chesterton, the beloved British author, was fond of speaking of God's laughter and he was boisterous in his own enjoyment of Christian life. He loved his conversion to the Church and seemed to smile his way to heaven. He was a combative defender of Christianity, but never with the leaden solemnity that marks many apologists and proponents of political correctness. He was a cheerful moralist.

I confess that I have barely touched the rich guidance of the *Catechism* on the role of grace and joy in Christian living. As Oscar Hammerstein wrote in *The Sound of Music*: "A song is no song till you sing it." Well, a life is not a life until you've lived it. The moral life is only a cheerless prospect to those who have not tried it. The moral life is a banquet, a feast the Lord invites us to join.

Growing in Faith

- Can you describe an experience of grace in your life?
- How does your practice of prayer affect your morals?
- Does the way you act influence the way you think and feel?

Growing in Knowledge

- What are the different names for Christ's New Law (*CCC*, 1965–1974)?
- What is the difference between acting out of love and acting out of fear?
- What wisdom do you sense in Joan of Arc's reply to her judges?
- Does original sin mean that people are basically bad? Review what the *Catechism* has to say on this topic (385–410).

CHAPTER TWO

Church as Mother and Teacher

A FLORENTINE ARTIST ONCE PRESENTED the pope with a painting entitled *The Bark of Peter*. The time was during the turmoil of the Protestant Reformation; the pope was Adrian VI. The painting was the artist's analogy of what the Church ought to be, especially in those troubled times: a Spanish galleon ship floating on a perfectly calm sea. No breeze stirred the flags and sails.

The artist pictured Pope Adrian kneeling on the deck with his hands folded and eyes lowered. Around him the cardinals stood in reverent silence. Below, in the staterooms, the laity peered through the portholes at the world. It was a scene of perfect order, quiet, self-assured and complacent. Around the edges of the painting, though, a storm raged. Rolling in this tempest of waves and lightning bolts were pagans, heretics, and unbelievers of every sort.

Pope Adrian studied the painting for a while and then gave an angry verdict. "This is not a picture of the true Church! A real Church must not leave the sheep without a shepherd. God's Church must be where the crisis is so that it may bring healing, love, justice, and mercy. Of course the Church contains the peace of Jesus in her heart, but she must be a mother to those in need and a teacher for those who hunger for truth."

Adrian pressed his fisherman's ring against the canvas where the "outcasts" were portrayed drowning in life's storms. "We must save and be saved with these, and these, and these! In the Gospel story of the storm at sea, Peter left the boat to walk on the stormy waters to Jesus. He sank in the waves because he needed more faith," exclaimed the pope. "But his heart was in the right place," continued Adrian. "After the graces of the Resurrection and Pentecost, Peter walked with people in life's storms and brought them Christ's salvation. He embodied the meaning of the Church as a mother and teacher."

The *Catechism*, echoing long tradition, speaks of the Church as our "Mother and Teacher" on matters of Christian living. The maternal image indicates the nurturing and affectionate interest the Church has in our moral and spiritual growth: "In her motherly care, the Church grants us the mercy of God which prevails over all our sins" (*CCC*, 2040).

The teaching image speaks of the Church as a trustworthy guide on moral issues. To live in Christ, we, the Church, must do three things, the *Catechism* tells us:

1. Link morality with our worship.
2. Appreciate the teaching authority (the magisterium) of Church leaders.
3. Become a missionary of moral witness.

We will explore these themes in this chapter.

Link Morality with Worship

The Church's liturgy offers the word, the sacraments, and the witness of the saints. Proclamation of the word teaches us the law of Christ, which is, above all, love of God and love of neighbor. "On these two commandments hang all the law and the prophets" (Matthew 22:40). The Eucharist and all the sacraments fill us with the grace and power of the Holy Spirit to help us in this call to Christian living. As the *Catechism* says, "The moral life is spiritual worship....The moral life finds its source and summit in the Eucharistic sacrifice" (*CCC,* 2031).

Through the Eucharist we participate in the great act of salvation that redeemed all of humanity: the dying and rising of Christ. Celebrating the Eucharist through the seasons of the Church year (Advent–Christmas, Lent–Easter–Pentecost, Ordinary Time) we die and we rise with Christ. We are made new again and again, joined to the new, redeemed creation, the kingdom of God, where love reigns.

The memorials and solemnities of the Blessed Mother and the saints show us examples of holiness. They remind us that others have responded to the call to holiness, and so can we. We are inspired to improve ourselves and learn virtue by hearing the stories of heroic lives.

The liturgy regularly celebrates the faith pilgrimage of saints who had been sinners. Scripture tells us that Mary Magdalene once hosted seven devils in her soul. Through the mercy of Jesus, she opened her heart to the seven gifts of the Holy Spirit. St. Augustine frankly confessed his life of youthful lust, as well as his fascination with false philosophies such as Manichaeism. Once Jesus touched him, he received a burning heart of pure divine love, and he converted his curious mind to serve the truth of the Gospel. St. Vincent de Paul hated being poor and became a clerical opportunist to assure himself a secure bankroll. After

Jesus captured his heart, Vincent plunged into a life of serving the poorest of the poor.

We usually see the successful side of the saints. We will find it reassuring to meditate on the process by which they became holy. Sanctity is a process that moves from sinfulness to holiness. That is the pilgrimage of grace celebrated in the Church's liturgy.

Nowhere is the Church more experienced as mother than in the liturgy. "With a mother's foresight, she lavishes on us day after day in her liturgy the nourishment of the word and Eucharist of the Lord" (*CCC*, 2040).

Appreciate the Church as Teacher

At the Last Supper, Jesus assured the apostles that he would form a Spirit-guided Church: "And I will ask the Father, and he will give you another Advocate, to be with you forever. This is the Spirit of truth, whom the world cannot receive, because it neither sees him nor knows him. You know him, because he abides with you, and he will be in you.... But the Advocate, the Holy Spirit, whom the Father will send in my name, will teach you everything, and remind you of all that I have said to you" (John 14:16–17, 26).

On Easter night Jesus appeared to the eleven apostles, gave them a greeting of peace and breathed on them, giving them the promised Holy Spirit. "Jesus said to them again, 'Peace be with you. As the Father has sent me, so I send you."... Receive the Holy Spirit" (John 20:21–22).

At the Ascension, Jesus commissioned the apostles to be teachers. "Go, therefore, and make disciples of all nations...teaching them to observe all that I have commanded you" (Matthew 28:19–20). This teaching office continues in the office of the popes and bishops and is called *magisterium*, from the Latin word for teacher. In moral matters, it is "ordinarily exercised in catechesis and preaching, with the help of the works of theologians and spiritual authors" (*CCC*, 2033).

Such leadership is needed, as the Church has always known.

Pope John Paul II was an outspoken moral leader. Indeed, many Church teachers and leaders are shining lights, pointing to the kind of moral leadership that reflects Church teaching and compassion. As president of the USCCB during the early 1990s, Cardinal William H. Keeler said this to his fellow bishops: "We in the Church stand with the unborn and the undocumented, the poor and the vulnerable, the hungry and the homeless in defense of human rights and human life. Our advocacy does not fit ideological or partisan categories, for our witness is not politically correct, but unfailingly consistent."

All of us in the Church must work together to create a moral society. "In the work of teaching and applying Christian morality, the Church needs the dedication of pastors, the knowledge of theologians, and the contributions of all Christians" and people of good will (*CCC*, 2038). Faith and the practice of the Gospel form each Catholic into life in Christ, an experience that causes in him or her a Spirit-guided sense of how to apply the divine moral law to the events of modern culture. "Thus the Holy Spirit can use the humblest to enlighten the learned and those in the highest positions" (*CCC*, 2038).

To live a moral life demands a proper formation of conscience. "Let your conscience be your guide" is authentic Catholic teaching. But it must be an *informed* and formed conscience. Conscience must be trained by the natural law, the Ten Commandments, the teachings of Christ, the instruction of the magisterium, and the inner working of the Spirit moving us to live in Christ.

Such a conscience is formed in the community of the Church. Hence it may not be a purely isolated, individual judgment of one's own acts apart from the common good. "I'll do it my way" just won't work. "Personal conscience and reason should not be set in opposition to the moral law or the magisterium of the Church" (*CCC*, 2039).

Jesus established the Church's teaching office to give us solid moral guidance. We can only have such assurance when we approach the Church's moral teachings in what St. Paul calls the "obedience of faith" (Romans 16:26). Reason alone is insufficient. It simply does not give us the rock-hard confidence we need. The author of the Epistle to the Hebrews tells us that faith is what endows us with "conviction and assurance" (see Hebrews 11:1). Reason tells us that "seeing is believing." Yet that is only half the story: Faith teaches us that "believing is seeing."

In our culture, so full of violence, promiscuity, abuse, and lies, obedient faith is indispensable for the recovery of a moral vision and moral behavior. The obedience of faith helps us to understand that the Church is a loving mother and a wise teacher.

In any healthy family, there are rules that set boundaries and allow the family to stay together and flourish. "Everyone must be home for supper five nights per week" might be one example. Although it is a rule which surely causes inconvenience at times, it safeguards the family.

Likewise, there are certain obligations that we, as Church, ask of each other. These precepts of the Church are spelled out in the *Catechism* (2041–2042). Flowing from a moral life and nourished by the liturgy, these positive laws are meant "to guarantee to the faithful the indispensable minimum in the spirit of prayer and moral effort, in the growth of love of God and neighbor." These precepts of the Church are:

You shall attend Mass on Sundays and holy days of obligation.

You shall confess your sins at least once a year.

You shall humbly receive your Creator in Holy Communion at least during the Easter season.

You shall keep holy the holy days of obligation.

You shall observe the prescribed days of fasting and abstinence.

Catholics also have the duty of providing for the material needs of the Church, each according to his or her abilities.

Become a Moral Missionary

Pope Paul VI often said that people today do not listen to teachers or preachers. They listen to witnesses: "Modern man listens more willingly to witnesses than to teachers, and if he does listen to teachers it is because they are witnesses" (On Evangelization in the Modern World, 41). Take the story of Nellie Sullivan, a Connecticut Latin teacher. She was an old-fashioned, strict schoolteacher. They used to say of her, "When girls go to her office for advice, they emerge as ladies."

Nellie was a daily communicant and believed that her constant contact with Jesus in the Mass and the sacraments was transforming her into Christ himself. She spent her summers going to Chicago and working on housing restoration projects for the poor. She could have worked in an office as an organizer, but she preferred scrubbing floors, painting walls, and cleaning sinks so that a poor family would have a nice place to stay. She said, "They are the giants and I am their servant." She kept this work a general secret from all but a few trusted friends.

When she retired and was too old and weak for such ministry, she became a volunteer at a local hospice. Every month she sent as many as one hundred handwritten letters to the relatives and friends of those who had died. Before Nellie herself died, she planned all the details of her funeral. Her theme was, "Come to the party. Rejoice in my journey to Christ." She ordered a floral display of cheerful yellow roses and said, "Don't put them on my coffin. Place them at the foot of the altar of the Bread of Life which has nourished me on my pilgrimage to God."

Nellie was a missionary to the poor and the dying as well as to her Latin students whose human dignity she fostered. "The witness of a Christian life and good works done in a supernatural spirit have great power to draw men to the faith and to God" (*CCC*, 2044). The moral teachings of the Church become credible and attractive when Catholics live and witness them. Or, as the *Catechism* says, "Because they are members of the Body whose head is Christ, Christians contribute to building up the Church by the constancy of their convictions and their moral lives" (*CCC*, 2045).

The word *martyr* means "witness." A martyr is the ultimate witness to the teachings of Christ. Can there be a greater love than to lay down your life for what you believe? St. Thomas More is one of the multitude of Christians who did. He was executed after choosing loyalty to his faith over loyalty to King Henry VIII. Thomas's love of the moral law was based on his love of the moral lawgiver. His faith connected the principle and the person.

We should become missionaries of Christ's moral teachings to our culture. Our witness, after all, makes the teaching believable to the people around us. It draws them to Jesus."

Growing in Faith

- Have you ever met a "moral missionary?" How did he or she influence people?
- How can the precepts of the Church nurture your sense of Catholic identity?
- What, in your opinion, is the most pressing moral need in our society today?
- Can you name a time when you were strengthened by grace to do the right thing?

Growing in Knowledge

- What is the role of personal conscience for Catholics?
- How is the Eucharist the summit of moral life?
- What is the magisterium? How is it exercised?
- Why do we call the Church "mother"?

CHAPTER THREE

Sin and Moral Sense

On December 14, 2012, twenty-year-old Adam Lanza fatally shot twenty children and six adult staff members in a mass murder at Sandy Hook Elementary School in the village of Sandy Hook in Newtown, Connecticut. Before driving to the school, Lanza had shot and killed his mother, Nancy, at their Newtown home. As first responders arrived, he committed suicide by shooting himself in the head.

The incident is the second-deadliest mass shooting by a single person in American history, after the 2007 Virginia Tech Massacre. It is the second-deadliest mass murder at an American elementary school, after the 1927 Bath School bombings.

The shootings prompted renewed debate about guns in the United States and a proposal for new legislation banning the sale and manufacture of certain types of semi-automatic firearms and magazines with more than ten rounds of ammunition.

There was more at stake in Newtown than a social sickness. Violence, murder, and revenge are indeed crimes and threats to public safety. But they are sins, too. Like all sins, they not only harm persons, but also violate the eternal laws of God. One of the great challenges of our day is that the awareness of sin has greatly diminished in our society. Yet sin remains. The denial of sin is a catastrophe, a moral defect.

Some years back, psychiatrist Karl Menninger wrote about this in his book *Whatever Became of Sin?* He wrote that we used to speak of sin as what was confessed to a priest. Unrepentant sinners could go to hell. Then we changed sin into a crime that was presented to a judge who committed the guilty to jail. Finally, we transformed sin into a neurosis, which we share with our therapist.

Menninger said we still have neuroses that are brought to the psychologist. We continue to have criminals who go to prison. But we have failed to keep alive an awareness of the reality of sin and legitimate moral guilt, as well as the power of absolution and the danger of hell. Our faith tells us there is a moral dimension to our acts as well as legal and therapeutic dimensions.

Yet our awareness of sin must take place in a context of grace. The *Catechism* discusses sin only after it has dealt with Christ's laws of love, the life of grace, the gifts of the Spirit, and the importance of virtue. That is why this book began with a reflection on grace and a meditation on the Church as our loving mother and teacher. The moral life, after all, is a response to God's love.

With this in mind let's see what the *Catechism* teaches about sin. I will highlight three directives of the *Catechism*:

1. Become aware of sin's meaning.
2. Avoid being entangled in sin's process.
3. Examine your conscience regularly.

Become Aware of Sin

"Sin is an offense against reason, truth and right conscience; it is failure in genuine love for God and neighbor.... It has been defined as 'an utterance, a deed or a desire contrary to the law of God'" (CCC, 1849).

Packed into these lines are the three major aspects of a sin: the rational, the relational, and the legal. Sin offends reason, truth, and conscience. Sin breaks loving relationships with God and others. Sin fractures the divine law. In all three cases, sin harms what is human about us. Sin diminishes us.

The definition of sin is simple, clear, and direct. But we need to recover what UCLA professor James Q. Wilson calls "the moral sense"—which is the title of his book on that topic and the source of his lifetime teachings. Wilson says that we must reawaken our consciousness of the reality of evil and the possibility of virtue, which he claims we have not lost completely.

Further, he raises the question of why bloodletting and savagery are news in this society, then offers two reasons. The first is because they are unusual: For most of us, our daily lives are not a war of all against all. Second, these types of events are still shocking. We continue to recoil in horror at pictures of starving children and death camp victims. Deep within us is an aversion to inhumanity. We have not totally lost our moral sense, but we do need to revive and nurture it. We will regain an appropriate awareness of sin when our moral sense is reborn.

At the heart of Wilson's concern is the family. Indeed, he describes his book as "in part an effort to explain the apparently irrational attachment of family members and to draw from those attachments the argument that they rest on a moral sense and a sketch of the way in which that sense develops."[2]

Our moral sentiments of sympathy, fairness, self-control, and conscientiousness are formed in the relationship we have with our parents. Given what Wilson describes as our natural sociability, these sentiments are innate; however, they appear and are developed only within "the routine intimacies of family life."[3] When we consciously undertake a daily pursuit of fairness, self-control, duty, loyalty, sympathy, love, and other virtues, our moral sense will mature along with the virtues.

How is this to be done? One of the best ways is the practice of virtues. One of the reasons why William J. Bennett's *Book of Virtues* remains a bestseller in the years since it was first published in 1996 is that Americans continue to hunger for a return to common sense and morality. Virtues are acquired by hearing stories that inspire us to virtuous behavior, seeing others practice these virtues, and undertaking a daily, serious commitment to the virtuous life. It may seem odd, but we will be more successful in arousing a sense of sin by practicing virtue than by a morose preoccupation with evil. Virtue training is one of the most effective ways to become aware of sin and have the strength to avoid it.

Happily, our faith tells us that we also have the graces of the sacraments (especially Eucharist and reconciliation) as well as the active presence of the seven gifts of the Holy Spirit (wisdom, understanding, counsel, fortitude, knowledge, piety, fear of the Lord) to help us conquer sin. And always before us is Jesus on the cross, offering us liberation from sin, and the risen Jesus, offering us the incomparable power of divine life, replacing the death of sin.

Avoid Sin's Entanglement

The *Catechism* echoes traditional teaching about mortal and venial sin: "Mortal sin destroys charity in the heart...by a grave violation of God's law." It turns one away from God, who is the ultimate end and beatitude, by preferring an inferior good to God. "For a sin to be mortal, three conditions must together be met: Mortal sin is sin whose object is a grave matter and which is also committed with full knowledge and deliberate consent" (*CCC*, 1855, 1857).

"One commits a venial sin, when in a less serious matter, [one] does not observe the standard prescribed by the moral law.... Venial sin does not deprive the sinner of sanctifying grace, friendship with God...and consequently eternal happiness" (*CCC*, 1862–1863).

The moral teachings of Jesus, the Ten Commandments, and the magisterium of the Church identify specific sins. Reflection on factors which influence knowledge and consent will determine our degree of moral accountability in a given act. The *Catechism* speaks of the entangling way sin can enter our lives: "Sin creates a proclivity to sin; it engenders vice by repetition of the same acts.... Sin tends to reproduce itself and reinforce itself, but it cannot destroy the moral sense at its root" (*CCC*, 1865).

I would offer a five-step process whereby sin can take hold of us and dull our moral sense:

1. The second sin is easier than the first.
2. The more we sin, the less we think we are sinning.
3. Veteran sinners begin to think that the sin is a virtue and virtue is a sin. In this upside-down morality, for example, teenagers involved in drugs and sex may intimidate the ones who abstain by claiming something is wrong with people who prefer chastity and a drug-free life.
4. Frequent sinning produces hostility to those striving to be moral. People trying honestly to live out the call of Christ often make sinners feel uncomfortable, not by any holier-than-thou condemnation, but simply by the goodness of their lives.

5. Committed sinners feel the pressure to attack, ridicule and undermine—even destroy—those struggling for goodness. Despite all the talk about tolerance, the committed sinners will not follow the principle of live and let live. At this point, evil and good are locked in mortal combat. Such was the drama of the passion of Christ. However, we should remember here Christ's first word from the cross, "Father, forgive them; for they do not know what they are doing" (Luke 23:34). Forgiveness is our healing response to those caught in the depth of sin.

This sketch of the sin process is meant to caution against the self-destructive behavior to which sin could lead us. It should also awaken us to the creative power of grace and forgiveness. One unforgettable example of forgiveness occurred when several Amish families showed the capacity to forgive the murder of five of their little daughters.

On October 2, 2006, in Nickel Mines, Pennsylvania, a neighbor who was a milkman walked into an Amish school house and lined up ten of the girls. He pulled out his gun and shot them all. Five died. The families picked up the bodies of their dead loved ones and brought them home. They removed the bloody clothes, and washed the bodies. Each re-clothed child was placed on a dining room table, and families sat around them in prayer and silence. Soon thereafter the parents visited the wife of the killer. They told her they have forgiven him. They asked permission to embrace her with reconciliation. They eventually shared with her some of the money sent worldwide to the Amish.

In their religious culture the Amish are trained to forgive those who offend them, insult their odd customs, ridicule their clothing, complain about their other worldly way of life—forgive even to the point when their children are slaughtered.

We can also mention here how in 1983 Pope John Paul II visited the jail cell of Ali Agca, who had attempted to assassinate the pope, in order to personally forgive him. After the visit the pope said, "I have fully forgiven him and I consider him to be a brother of mine."

Examine Your Conscience

In our psychologically sensitive culture we are easily led to examine our subconscious. This has its own value inasmuch as it tries to find out our hidden motives or the unresolved emotional problems from our past life. But there is age-old wisdom in the Church, summed up by St. Augustine at the turn of the fifth century: "Return to your conscience. Question it.... Turn inward, brethren, and in everything you do, see God as your witness" (*CCC*, 1779).

We should examine consciousness—our conscience—as well as the subconscious. Taking an honest look at ourselves each day affords the opportunity for regular self-improvement. Many people miss its advantages by three common forms of escapism.

First, some kill their consciences by convincing themselves they have nothing to feel guilty about. They deny the reality of sin and believe they are beyond good and evil. They have somehow arrived at the position that all their choices are self-legitimating. Whatever they decide becomes correct simply in the choosing.

Others drown out conscience's voice beyond hearing. It is as though they stroll through life with earphones cemented to their ears, pounding music closing off all self-examination. They may use sex, drink, drugs, or work to run away from the voice of conscience.

Third, some deny what their consciences try to tell them. These people rationalize all their behavior. They refuse responsibility for their errant behavior and blame the culture, the politicians, the economy, family background, or the Church instead. They falsely assume they can never be self-directed.

It has been said that the unexamined life is not worth living. If so, then the examined life contains much promise for those who have discovered its benefits. Spiritual writers have offered many ways to examine our consciences.

The technique called "the Parade of the Night" is one useful way to approach self-examination. At the end of the day, try visualizing the faces of all the people you have met that day. As each face comes into focus, reflect upon what your encounter was like. Use these or similar questions: How did I treat each person I met? Indifferently? Patronizingly? Did I put on a show? Did I pretend to have emotions I did not feel? Was I outwardly friendly but hostile inside? Was I kind? Did I make them happy? Was I generous with my time?

Conversely, how did others treat me? Were they cold? Did they refuse to listen to me? Did they make me feel I was a nothing? If so, what did I do? What should I do? When Christ came to me in them, did I recognize him? How much did prayer mean for my relationships? How strongly did faith affect my relationships with others? What have I learned for tomorrow's encounters?

Shakespeare said, "Conscience doth make cowards of us all" (*Hamlet,* Act 3, Scene 1) Perhaps, but a good conscience doth make honest people out of us and is so soft a pillow that we can always expect a good night's rest.

Christian Balance

I said at the beginning of this chapter that we should keep sin and grace together. Original sin teaches us that human nature is radically flawed. Grace reminds us that human nature is radically redeemed. That balance helps us understand ourselves and people in general. It allows us to be realists without becoming cynical. Grace, which will triumph, tempers our knowledge that there is a lot of sin in the world. On the other hand, sin tempers any illusions we have that everything will be perfect on this earth. A balanced outlook allows us to be optimists without illusions.

The *Catechism* captures this balanced vision, helping us avoid a morbid sin-and-guilt religion weighed down with rules and laws, though appreciating the role of guilt and law. It rescues us, too, from a rosy, feel-good religion that imagines there is no sin, that guilt is best left to therapists and absolved by a sedative. Christ's grace is a free gift, the very life of God, "infused by the Holy Spirit into our soul to heal it of sin and to sanctify it" (*CCC*, 1999). Health and self-fulfillment can be found in this Catholic vision of balance between grace and sin.

Growing in Faith

- How does practicing virtue make you more aware of sin?
- Why should we think of sin in the context of grace?
- Do you agree that society has lost its moral sense? Why or why not?
- Name how guilt can be both good and bad.

Growing in Knowledge

- How does a deepening relationship with Christ keep you from sinning?
- What methods do you use to examine your conscience?
- What are the three ways in which sin diminishes us?
- In what three ways do we acquire virtue?

CHAPTER FOUR

Love God

What do you say about a twenty-four-year-old nun who died of tuberculosis? In the case of St. Thérèse of Lisieux, plenty. But that wasn't the opinion of her Carmelite sisters who commented outside her sickroom: "Thérèse will die soon. What will the prioress write in her obituary? 'She entered our convent, lived, and died.' There is really no more to say." Yet within a few months of her death such a storm of interest and affection for Thérèse began that a Vatican cardinal declared, "We must hasten to canonize Thérèse, otherwise we shall be anticipated by the voice of the people."

What accounted for the enormous public interest in Thérèse? It was the publication of her spiritual journal, *The Story of a Soul*. The book became an immediate bestseller worldwide and revealed her story—a message that has touched millions ever since. Her advice is simplicity itself: What is important is not great deeds, but to do everyday acts with great love for God and neighbor. "I will return to earth to teach people to love Love," she wrote. Her love of God was absolute. It found practical expression in love of people.

Love of God and people sums up the moral life. The Ten Commandments (also called the Decalogue) reflect this teaching. The *Catechism* comments, "When someone asks him, 'Which commandment of the Law is the greatest?' Jesus replies, 'You shall love the Lord your God with all your heart, and with all your soul and with all your mind. This is the greatest and first commandment. And a second is like it: You shall love your neighbor as yourself.' The Decalogue must be interpreted in the light of this twofold, yet single commandment of love" (*CCC*, 2055).

The first three commandments are about love of God; the last seven deal with love of people. In this chapter we will see how the love of God is expressed in the first two commandments: "Worship the Lord your God, and serve only him" (Matthew 4:10; see also Exodus 20:2–5) and "You shall not make wrongful use of the name of the Lord your God." (Exodus 20:7). Those commandments call us to do three things:

1. Listen to love's lesson.
2. Give up false gods.
3. Search for the sacred.

We'll conclude with some practical advice from Jesus.

Listen to Love's Lesson

The Bible often teaches through pictures; think of Mount Sinai and Mount Calvary and of the Upper Room. At Sinai God said, "I bore you on eagles' wings and brought you to myself. Now therefore, if you obey my voice and keep my covenant, you shall be my treasured possession out of all the peoples" (Exodus 19:4–5). Once God and Israel are bound in love, then the commandments are given as signs of how to love.

At Calvary Jesus consummated the greatest act of love in history and saved the world from its sins. In the Upper Room Jesus gave us the Eucharist, the supreme sacrament of love. In that same

Upper Room, the Holy Spirit came at Pentecost, the Person of perfect love between the Father and the Son. In all these high places pictures are given of the dialogue of salvation between God and people. God offers us love and invites us to return that love. It is the essence of morality.

We all know we should love people, yet some people forget we should love God. If we stop loving God, we will stop loving people. We will also lose faith and hope in God. "The First Commandment embraces faith, hope and love" (*CCC*, 2086), observes the *Catechism*. And again, "Faith in God's love encompasses the call and the obligation to respond with sincere love to divine charity" (*CCC*, 2093).

The easiest way to have faith in God is to love him. St. Teresa of Avila urges, "Habitually make many acts of love of God, for they set the soul on fire and make it gentle."[4] A faith crisis is usually a love crisis.

When we fail to love God we will lose our hope in him. Fear will take over our lives. The vacuum of love is always filled with fear. People who read the Ten Commandments with no love of God in their hearts will see them as tenets of fear and hate them. Love is letting go of fear. "There is no fear in love, but perfect love casts out fear." (1 John 4:18).

St. Bernard of Clairvaux taught that there are four stages in developing a love for God:

I love myself for my own sake. I am self-centered and have no interest in God.

I become aware of God and of my dependence on him, but I still love God for my own sake; I only turn to God to fulfill my needs. In most cases this second stage comes about through a vivid awareness of Jesus.

I begin to love God for his sake. I experience an attraction to God in worship, meditation, and prayer. God's love for me becomes apparent and heartwarming. A personal relationship with Jesus becomes a powerful incentive.

I love myself solely for the sake of God. Now I best appreciate my origin and destiny in God. I am humbled by the incredible gift of divine love and feel my whole life has importance because of God.

The reason we can embark on this love journey is because God is always calling us with love, and because God has put within us the capacity to respond. "The First Commandment enjoins us to love God above everything and all creatures for him and because of him" (*CCC*, 2093).

Give Up False Gods

The positive virtues called for by the First Commandment are faith, hope, and love regarding God. This commandment also forbids certain kinds of behavior: superstition, idolatry, magic (not the sleight-of-hand entertainment kind), sacrilege, simony (the buying or selling of spiritual things and offices), atheism, and agnosticism (*CCC*, 2110–2132).

In all of these behaviors, there is a denial of a living and loving God. Idolatry today is worship of sex, money, or power. Sacrilege is a loss of the sense of the sacred. We will look at this more closely in a moment. But the commandment to resist irreligion—that is, tempting God in word or deed, sacrilege, or simony—calls for some special comment.

Atheists and agnostics today wear the face of secular humanism. They want to strip from public life (government, law, education, entertainment, medicine, workplace) all signs and teachings of religion and faith. Religion's opponents use the media to teach their anti-gospel. They resort to the legislatures and courts to enforce their views in society. In my view, they pervert the privileges of freedom to purge religion from life. Some atheists and agnostics may be sincere, but sincerity is no excuse for the damage such irreligion creates in society.

We of the Church are commanded to resist the encroachments of irreligion. The best response to irreligion is revitalizing faith among believers. Some say, "Fight fire with fire," meaning "Engage the enemy in the public square using the media, the courts, and the law, only more effectively than they do." Did not Jesus say that we should learn from the wisdom of this world, for the children of the world are wiser than the children of light?

Obviously, there is room for public engagement: Responsible believers will become involved in the struggle. But the prior condition for success is to set faith on fire in homes and parishes across the land. Personal and communal faith, both believed and witnessed with enthusiasm, is a force that could swamp irreligion if we had the will. Once we have the will, we will discover the means. In a battle of two opposing forces of equal strength, the side with the will to win prevails.

Of course such growth in faith is not just a matter of gritty human determination. It always involves joyous dependence on the grace of God. Prayer, worship, and adoration are the lifeblood of faith growth. Only with God's help will our faith be living, conscious, and active.

St. Francis de Sales said, "Divine love not only commands us again and again to love our neighbor, but itself produces the love as its own image and likeness and sheds it over our hearts."[5] He linked the love of God with faith life. He felt compassion for the culture of his day and regretted that so many people were sheep without a shepherd. He would love them into faith. "We bishops must be like those large drinking fountains, where all have the right to come for water."[6] The same is true for each of us. We can avoid false gods and counter irreligion by starting with an ardent love of God.

Search for the Sacred

The positive message of the Second Commandment is this: Value the sacredness of the person, the holiness of God, the sanctity and mystery of life and creation.

Love and reverence are synonymous: "The sense of the sacred is part of the virtue of religion.... The Second Commandment prescribes respect for the Lord's name.... God calls each one by name"(*CCC*, 2144, 2142). In baptism, we link our own name to God's: "Everyone's name is sacred. It demands respect as the sign of the one who bears it" (*CCC*, 2158).

It is no secret that much of the entertainment world—especially movies, plays, novels, and popular music—has become coarse, vulgar, uncivilized, and blasphemous in thought, word, and deed. The sense of the sacred has vanished from most productions. The art world, both in photography and painting, is following suit. Even ads are pushing the edges.

Yet those we love we treat with respect and reverence. We hold them sacred, we speak their names with affection. Freedom of speech in America is a precious right, but that right is endangered when it is abused and exploited.

This Second Commandment forbids behavior that insults and wounds the sacred: It "forbids the abuse of God's name, that is, every improper use of the names of God, Jesus Christ, but also of the Virgin Mary and all the saints" (*CCC*, 2146). Blasphemy is contrary to the respect due to God and his holy name: "It is... blasphemous to make use of God's name to cover up criminal practices, to reduce people to servitude, to torture prisoners or put them to death" (*CCC*, 2148). We should also include in this list false oaths and perjury.

A feeling for the reality of the sacred has been captured by the film, *Of Gods and Men*, directed by Xavier Beauvois. The film won the Grand Prix Award and two other best film awards. It was a commercial and critical success. It is the story of contemplative monks in highlands of Algeria, how they lived and served the local Muslim community and eventually were martyred by local authorities. The film manages to communicate the reality of prayer, union with God, and a respect for the sacred, while at the same time serving the poor and the sick.

The following film review, written by Roland Krundt and published in the September 9, 2012, issue of *The New Yorker* magazine, is a tribute to these values.

> Few of us are personally acquainted with renunciants, the monks and nuns who have renounced worldly attachments to serve God. They are worth knowing. *Of Gods and Men* provides a relatively easy entré, with no need to shave your head or disavow your iPhone.
>
> Based on a true story, *Of Gods and Men* observes a community of eight French Trappist monks in remote Algeria. They become pawns in a violent political game. Their lives are explicitly at risk. Eventually, after much soul-searching, they accept that risk rather than prudently returning to France. In the end, most of them are kidnapped and—mercifully off screen, after the movie ends—beheaded.
>
> By testing the monks' faith with physical peril, the movie

> explores what faith is and what it means. Although the plot is sensational, the movie is contemplative. The final shot is unforgettable: Accompanied by their captors, the monks march uphill through an African snowfall; just as the colors gradually fade into shades of grey, the image of the departing monks quietly dissolves into the surrounding dark. See it if you dare.

Pope Francis presents a view of the sacred that is simple, humble, and accessible. After he was named pope, when he appeared on the balcony of St. Peter's he just wore a simple white cassock. He bowed his head and begged the throng to bless him. Only after that did he offer them his blessing.

Francis lives in simple quarters at St. Martha's hotel instead of a royal apartment in the Vatican palace. His daily sermons are published worldwide each day and impress us with his earthy, practical meaning of the Gospels. We are not canonizing him with these portraits, but are affirming that Pope Francis has found the presence of our Holy God in the simple facts of daily life. He fulfills the meaning of the Second Commandment.

Practical Advice from Jesus

The simplest way to have a spiritual journey and get in touch with the sacred is to pray. People who pray will not blaspheme, curse, perjure themselves, or pollute the air with obscenities. Take a look at John's Gospel for some practical guidance on prayer. Read the stories of the raising of Lazarus (11:33–44); the prediction of the agony at Gethsemane (12:27–33); the expulsion of Judas (13:21–31). All these stories show Jesus praying, going through four steps.

1. He begins by being "troubled in spirit." At Bethany he mourns for Lazarus. At Gethsemane he trembles with a natural fear of death. In the Upper Room he regrets the betrayal of a friend.
2. He brings this experience into a communion with his Father. Scripture remains quiet before this mystery of his communion, does not analyze it, but acknowledges its presence.
3. There is an answer to Christ's prayer. Yes, Lazarus will live again. No, the cup of suffering cannot pass. Judas betrays Jesus.
4. An acceptance of the Father's will combines with an act of adoration. All three stories end with Christ's adoration, glorifying the Father's name.

Jesus's four-step example of prayer is for our lives, too. Often "troubled in spirit," we should live with a consciousness of God's presence. Hence our human experience should always have a divine light shining on it. Second, we should bring our life experience to a time of meditation and communion with God. Like Jesus, we must "go aside." Deliberate meditation time opens us to a deeper awareness of God and conversation with God.

Third, we await an answer. Here recall that Jesus experienced joy at Bethany, sorrow at Gethsemane, and regret in the Upper Room. Our feelings are secondary to God's will. We seek the God of consolations—not the consolations of God. Finally, we must surrender to God's decision with peace and with profound adoration. As Jesus says in John's Gospel, "Father, glorify your name" (12:28).

This brief lesson on prayer is but one of many to be found in Scripture and spiritual writings. Prayer is the perfect antidote to the skin-deep coarseness of our day.

Other practical advice builds on the positive goals of the Second Commandment, the goals of respect for God and neighbor. To parents, this commandment is a reminder to watch your tongue. Civil and respectful talk among adults sets the tone for the children.

Teachers, purge any cynicism that may creep into your lectures and dialogues. Employers, think of restoring a workplace filled with the fresh air of good English, words that build up people and traditional beliefs. Entertainers, recover the art of making people laugh without putting others down. Make us smile at folly in a gentle, human way. When we love God and treat others with respect, we will be happy and bring joy to others. That loving union with God and neighbor is the goal of the moral life.

Growing in Faith

- Who are the false gods in my life and what should I do about them?
- What are three ways I could get in touch with the sacred in my life?
- How would I share my spiritual journey with others?
- What are some strategies for promoting religious values in public life?

Growing in Knowledge

- What way of praying can we learn from the Gospel of John?
- What are some key teachings of our consumer culture? What is the best way to respond?
- Do you see signs in our society of greater interest in things spiritual? If so, what are they?

CHAPTER FIVE

Rediscover the Christian Sabbath

One of Norman Rockwell's most beloved paintings was titled *Sunday Morning*, and it appeared on the cover of the May 19, 1959, edition of the *Saturday Evening Post*. In it he depicted a mother and her three children, well dressed and heading for church. On a chair in front of them is dad holding the Sunday paper, with sections of the paper scattered around him on the floor. Even in those days absenteeism from Sunday church attendance was common, though not as prevalent as it is today.

By now most people know that Catholic Mass attendance has declined, a fact that is worrying bishops and pastors. The Center for Applied Research in the Apostolate (CARA) at Georgetown University conducted research on this movement, which was published in a report issued by the National Association for Lay Ministry in 2011.

The report indicated that 23 percent of self-identified adult Catholics attend Mass *every* week. Yet, in *any given* week, 31 percent of Catholics are attending Mass (almost identical to the 30-percent estimate from research by the Gallup organization). There is considerable geographic variation in Mass attendance levels across the country, with higher levels in the Midwest and lower levels in coastal urban areas. During Lent and Advent, Mass attendance increases into the mid-40 percent range and on Christmas and Easter, an estimated sixty percent of Catholics attend.[7]

Thus, if one is seeking to make a comparison of Mass attendance in the 1950s to now, the drop is from a peak of 62 percent in 1958 to about 31 percent now. This is a remarkable decline. It means that the Mass attendance you see at Christmas and Easter is a lot like the attendance you might have seen in a typical week in the late 1950s. Yet, even then, as now, there were a significant number of Catholics like the father in Rockwell's *Sunday Morning* who chose to do something else.

The solution to this pastoral challenge is not easy. In this chapter we can list hints of an approach that, with God's graces and a surge of faith in our people, can reverse this situation.

The *Catechism of the Catholic Church* explains that commitment to religion and worship resonates with the teaching of the Third Commandment: "Remember the sabbath day, and keep it holy. Six days you shall labor and do all your work. But the seventh day is a sabbath to the Lord your God; you shall not do any work" (Exodus 20:8–10; cf. Deuteronomy 5:12–14). We honor this commandment by resting from our ordinary labors and worshiping God" (*CCC*, 2168).

There are three keys to the *Catechism* teaching on observing the sabbath:

1. Honor the day of rest.
2. Understand why Sunday Eucharist is essential.
3. Participate more fully in the Eucharist.

Be Renewed by Rest

In the early days of the Industrial Revolution sweatshops abounded in our big cities where men, women, and children—many of whom were immigrants—worked fifteen hours a day, sometimes seven days a week, in horrible and unsafe workplaces for slave wages. Of the money made, 80 percent was spent on food, most of it bread and potatoes, once in a while a cabbage. There was no health care or possibility of saving money to buy a house.

"Not only was this a terrible social injustice to these unfortunate people, it also denied them the regular time they needed to regain their strength and renew their human dignity." Most of them were helpless to defend themselves, unable to speak English, and terrified of deportation. They deserved a living wage for their families and time to restore their health.

For these workers, rest and relaxation were denied them by their employers. Yet even though laws have changed and working conditions improved for most people who work in the first world today, millions of people in our culture freely deny themselves time to relax. The workaholism so characteristic of consumer society means that Sunday is never a day of rest—even for the majority of those who do not need to work to maintain services for the public good (police, firefighters, medical personnel, and so on).

Back in the early 1990s, author Witold Rybczynski chronicled this cultural shift in his book *Waiting for the Weekend*: "Where once the week consisted of weekdays and Sunday," now it is weekdays and the weekend. "Ask most people to name the first day of the week and they will answer 'Monday, of course'; fifty years ago the answer would have been Sunday."[8] Then as now, for many people the weekend is busier and more exhausting than workdays. For many Sunday is neither a day of rest nor a day for worship.

The *Catechism* teaches otherwise: "God's action is the model for human action. If God 'rested and was refreshed' on the seventh day," we, too, "ought to 'rest' and should let others, especially the poor, 'be refreshed.' The sabbath brings everyday work to a halt and provides a respite. It is a day of protest against the servitude of work and the worship of money" (*CCC*, 2172).

The wisdom of the Third Commandment is that life should be a rhythm of work and rest. Without the work break, we become a stressed-out society with all the well-known tension-related diseases. God made us and knows what is best for our human development. While God cannot grow tired and needs no rest in the strict sense of the word, even God rested on the seventh day to give us the example (Genesis 2:2).

Our weekly day off should give us perspective on the meaning and value of what we do, and help us to see our lives against the backdrop of the bigger picture. It is a day for looking at creation—and the Creator from whom all these blessings flow. It is a day for more relaxed time with family and friends, a day for reading and cultural activities, a day for leisure in the highest sense of that word. From this viewpoint the Third Commandment is part of our health plan, the breather that restores our vitality. It is also essential to our spirituality.

Sunday Eucharist Is Essential

Sabbath means "rest" and refers to the seventh day of the week. In Christianity, the sabbath observance was moved to Sunday because it was on the first day of the week that Jesus rose from the dead and inaugurated the new creation. Jesus witnessed and shared with us our call to an eternal sabbath and rest in God.

"The celebration of Sunday observes the moral commandment inscribed by nature in the human heart to render to God an outward, visible, public, and regular worship 'as a sign of his universal beneficence to all,'" says the *Catechism*. "Sunday worship fulfills the moral command of the Old Covenant, taking up its rhythm and spirit in the weekly celebration of the Creator and Redeemer of his people" (CCC, 2176).

Catholics properly celebrate Sunday by participating in the Holy Eucharist. "The Sunday celebration of the Lord's Day and his Eucharist is at the heart of the Church's life.... This practice of the Christian assembly dates from the beginnings of the apostolic age [see Acts 2:42–46]." It is reflected in an ancient sermon: "'Come to Church early, approach the Lord, and confess your sins, repent in prayer.... Be present at the sacred and divine liturgy, conclude in prayer and do not leave before the dismissal'" (CCC, 2177–2178).

In times past, parents often motivated the children to go to Mass by reminding them of those who were forbidden to have Mass. The power of Eucharistic celebration also seems stronger when one is in danger of death. Following is an excerpt from a letter written by a soldier during the Persian Gulf War:

> Last week God tested my faithfulness to him. I had just arrived at our new position in the desert. Each of us had to dig our fighting holes. My platoon sergeant came and said, "Sunday Mass is at 5 p.m." I thanked him. I was tired but I still wanted to go to Mass. About 4:45 p.m. it started to rain

> pretty bad. The wind made it more uncomfortable. Then I heard the bell for Mass. "Well," I said to myself, "this is a test of your faithfulness to God." Then the devil said to me, "If you go out there, you are going to get all wet and you will be miserable." I grabbed my hat and headed for Mass. After Mass, I was wet and cold and had no dry clothes to change into. See, I thought about it and said, "If God sacrificed his body for me, I shouldn't mind getting wet at all."[9]

Love and Live the Eucharist

We fulfill our worship obligation by participating in the Eucharistic celebration either on the Sunday or a holy day of obligation, or on the evening before: "'On Sundays and other holy days of obligation the faithful are bound to participate in the Mass.'... The Sunday Eucharist is the foundation and confirmation of all Christian practice" (*CCC*, 2180–2181).

We should view the Third Commandment's obligation more as a privilege and joy than simply as a law. When we love the Mass we do not think of it in terms of burden or obligation. Love moves to the beloved with light wings, not with leaden feet.

The best way to love the Mass is to live the Mass. Consider the four steps in the prayers of consecration, which repeat what Jesus did at the Last Supper. There, Jesus takes, blesses, breaks, and gives the bread that has been transformed into his body. But he does more than say those words: he lives them. He surrenders himself to the Father who takes him like a shepherd takes a lamb from the flock. Then the Father consecrates him, blesses him for the coming sacrifice of the cross. Third, the Father releases him to be broken on the cross. Last, the Father gives Jesus to the world as the Bread of Life.

Jesus freely allows himself to be taken. Had he so willed, he could have called on legions of angels to save him. He bows before the blessing of the Father and accepts his consecration to mission. Jesus offers his whole being and body to be broken on the cross. Jesus becomes the Living Bread, baked in the fire of suffering and death, for the life of the world.

This is the four-step Eucharistic model for us that puts the sabbath at the center of our lives. In Mass after Mass we have the opportunity to be taken by God for God's service. We surrender in joy to the Father's will. We identify with the words of the Mass that beg the Holy Spirit to come and bless and change the bread in the divine fire. We too need the blessing fire of the Spirit to give us the divine outlook on the world and prepare us for sacrificial love. Like the bread, as individuals and as a community, we need to be transformed.

Third, we offer our bodies to be broken: our personhood to be placed at the service of total love of God and neighbor with all the crosses this will involve. Last, we exult in the knowledge we can now be given to the world as the bread of love, justice, and mercy for others.

Here is a prayer that you may find helpful:

> O Jesus, see the world with my eyes. Hear the world with my ears. Speak to people with my mouth. Touch people with my hands. Love others with my heart. Walk in my feet that I my bear your presence wherever I go. Make my whole being a transparency of your presence.

How can our participation in the Holy Eucharist be made more effective? Try these suggestions.

1. Obtain a book that has the weekly readings for each Sunday and feast day of the liturgical year, for the purpose of meditating on the readings before Mass. You can also find this information online at www.usccb.org. Everywhere else in life, people get ready for meetings by reading over the agenda and related materials beforehand. We should do the same for Mass. If we arrive with some prayerful knowledge about the readings, the theme of the Sunday, and the mood of the liturgical season, we will bring an intelligent faith to the liturgy. Our minds will be open to what God wants to say to us at worship.
2. Arrive at Mass with an attitude of giving oneself to the celebration. Come with ears open to God's word, eyes open to the beauty of the ritual, throat open to sing and pray with all our strength, and a heart open to give all the love we can to God. Some come to Mass and complain, "I get nothing out of it." But we only get what we give. If at the end of the Mass we can say, "I loved God with all my heart; I loved God with all my mind; I loved God with all my strength"; then we will indeed "get a lot out of Mass."
3. Open yourself to the spirit of community at Mass. The Eucharist is not for loners. At the Last Supper, the one loner was Judas, the secret agent at the table. He had made his private arrangements for the betrayal of Jesus. He never understood how to be part of the apostolic community. Jesus expelled him from the Lord's Supper, but Judas had already exiled himself internally. Jesus simply confirmed what Judas

had done to himself. The Eucharist is a celebration of love. True love requires a relationship with others. The Mass, of course, is also a sacrifice. Entering into the Eucharistic community demands a sacrifice from us. The trade-off is most satisfying, for only in self-sacrifice does true self-fulfillment occur.

4. Come to Eucharist with a soul full of prayer. The more deeply we have learned how to pray always, morning, noon, and night, the more the Mass will be a joy to us, for the Eucharist is the summit of prayer. The Mass completes, perfects, and reenergizes our prayer so that our journey with Christ becomes evermore intimate throughout our lives.

These four commonsense guidelines can make all the difference in our participation in Sunday Eucharist. They turn a law into love, a burden into a sweet experience, a mystery into an hour of light at the beginning—but really at the center—of our week.

I close with some comments on Mass attendance and parish membership from Msgr. Charles Pope, a pastor in Washington, DC, in a blog post he wrote on *New Advent*, a daily collection of blogs on Catholic issues:

> Will we see growth in the numbers in our pews each Sunday? But the key question is, will it hold steady or grow? Or will it drop further? That surely depends on us evangelizing and working to restore people to the Sacraments! It may also be affected by other things such as the economy, the emergence (or not) of some significant crisis and so forth. A final factor that is probably hard to gauge is what happens to the children and grandchildren of non-practicing Catholics? Will

they continue to self-identify as Catholics or will that "identity" fade as the generations proceed? It's hard to know.

Thus, while the overall news of a growing Catholic population looks good, there are on-going questions about how many of them will, in any meaningful way, practice the Catholic faith and/or hand it on to their children and grandchildren. I have long thought that we too quickly admire the numbers present in megachurches and have long suspected that they don't keep their members for a long time. I have a lot of anecdotal evidence that people go for a year or so and eventually get bored or disillusioned and move on to another megachurch, then to another. At some point they leave the system altogether and I thus suspect the megachurch phenomenon will run its course and the numbers overall will diminish in that "branch of Zion."

But there is good news here if we compare ourselves to other churches. However, it is still an awful fact that one-third of those raised Catholic later leave the Church and lose the sacraments. This is still an awful number.

Growing in Faith

- Describe an experience when rest renewed your faith.
- How can you participate more fully in Sunday Mass?
- What can you do to make Sunday more a day of rest and renewal?

Growing in Knowledge

- What is the symbolism of the Sabbath to the life of a Christian?
- Why did Christians move the sabbath to Sunday?
- Why is Sunday Eucharist essential for Catholics?

CHAPTER SIX

Family Values

> "Marriage and family are ordered to the good of the spouses, to the procreation and education of the children.... Children owe their parents respect, gratitude, just obedience, and assistance."
>
> (CCC, 2249, 2251)

THE FOURTH COMMANDMENT DEALS WITH all aspects of family life—filial and parental duties and responsibilities. It also speaks to the state and the society what they need to do to foster authentic family values and strengthen the whole family in every way possible.

We have seen how the first three commandments show us to love God with our hearts and strength. The next seven commandments show us how to love others as we love ourselves.

The Fourth Commandment lays out the duties of parents to their children, the responsibilities of children to their parents, and the care of adult children to their aging parents. This commandment also refers to one's relationship to those who exercise authority: teachers, leaders, and those who govern our communities.

The commandments that follow the fourth deal with other aspects that affect family life: the role of marriage, respect for life, attitudes to material goods, the commitment to truth, concern for the poor, dedication to justice as a requisite for peace.

The African proverb, "It takes a village to raise a child" has been oft-repeated in the last twenty years, especially since the publication, in 1996, of Hillary Rodham Clinton's book *It Takes a Village*. The image evokes nostalgic memories of storybook families in quiet rural settings or in yeasty ethnic neighborhoods from the distant American past: two-parent families, two sets of grandparents, and lots of aunts, uncles, cousins, and neighbors close at hand.

The spiritual heart of these towns and urban neighborhoods was the church or synagogue, with strong support from the local parochial or public school. Garrison Keillor recovers that vision with gentle humor in his Prairie Home Companion radio sketches from the fictional town of Lake Wobegon. There, he jests, "All the women are strong, all the men are good-looking, and all the children are above average."

We like to think of days when children were taught obedience and respect for parents, adults, and public leaders; when the elderly were cared for at home, mostly; when fathers trained (and civilized) their sons and mothers nurtured their daughters. For some, these idyllic scenes were true. For others, childhood may have been a painful and unhappy time. Most, though, can think back on family experiences removed from these extremes.

Village and neighborhood family life of earlier generations was not perfect, and rarely happened the way we imagine it. Yet our idealized picture symbolizes the love and closeness we all long for. The Fourth Commandment—and those that follow—speaks to the family and civic virtues we need to achieve the happiness, fulfillment, and peace that God wants for us. "Honor your father and your mother" is the commandment in Deuteronomy 5:16. After God, "we should honor our parents to whom we owe life and who have handed on to us the knowledge of God" (CCC, 2197).

The *Catechism* shows how, through our faith, we can live close to the ideals of family closeness that our hearts desire. In this chapter we'll highlight three important actions we can take:

1. Renew the ideal of the Christian family.
2. Honor our parents.
3. Support the principles in the family Bill of Rights.

Renew the Ideal

"A man and a woman united in marriage, together with their children, form a family.... The relationships within the family bring an affinity of feelings, affections and interests, arising from all the members' respect for one another.... Authority, stability, and a life of relationships within the family constitute the foundations of freedom, security and fraternity within society" (CCC, 2202, 2206, 2207).

The *Catechism*'s truths about the family confront the tragic breakdown of family life in America. On the positive side, our culture is finally waking up to the need to save marriage and the family.

According to the U.S. Census Bureau, twenty-four million children in America—one out of three—live in homes where the biological father is absent. Consequently, there is a father factor in nearly all of the social issues facing America today. Numerous studies have focused on the negative effects of father absence on poverty, maternal and child health, incarceration, crime, teen pregnancy, child abuse, drug and alcohol abuse, education, and childhood obesity.

The data also tells us that children in father-absent homes are almost four times more likely to be poor. In 2011, 12 percent of children in married-couple families were living in poverty, compared to 44 percent of children in mother-only families.[10]

In the 2009 edition of *State of Our Unions*, an annual report issued by the National Marriage Project at the University of Virginia and the Institute for American Values, statistics about marriage, economics, and self-reported happiness collected over the last forty years were culled to create a portrait of the ways in which American couples are thriving and the problems—new and old—they face. W. Bradford Wilcox, a sociology professor at the university, is the director of the National Marriage Project. He says that protecting marriage is critically important to the health of our society:

> First and foremost, children tend to do best when they are reared in homes headed by married parents. For instance, boys are half as likely to end up in trouble with the law if they are raised by both of their married parents. Second, adults who form and maintain successful marriages over the course of their lives are much more likely to enjoy healthy, wealthy and happy lives than are their peers who do not get and stay successfully married.

One organization that is helping to restore the institution of marriage is Marriage Savers, founded by Mike McManus and his wife, Harriet. The group has helped over ten thousand clergy create Community Marriage Policies in 229 cities over twenty-five years. These cities have subsequently reduced their divorce rates by an average of over 17 percent in seven years, cut cohabitation rates by a third over a decade, and raised marriage rates.[11]

In 2008, Mike and Harriet coauthored a book titled *Living Together: Myths, Risks & Answers*, in which they suggest a strategy any church could use to reduce cohabitation before marriage. Also in 2008, Mike wrote a book called *How to Cut America's Divorce Rate in Half*. Stories about Marriage Savers have appeared on CBN's 700 Club and ABC World News. Mike has been a guest on *Oprah*, *O'Reilly*, *NBC Nightly News*, *CBS Early Show* and *48 Hours*, and *Focus on the Family*.

In an article that appears on the website of the Catholic News Agency, "Five Myths about No-Fault Divorce," author Stephen Baskerville outlines some of the most common clichés and misconceptions about modern divorce, along with the facts.

> Myth 1: *No-fault divorce permitted divorce by mutual consent, thus making divorce less acrimonious.*
> Fact: No-fault divorce is unilateral divorce. It permits divorce by one spouse acting alone for any reason or no reason. It is therefore forced divorce, meaning you can be divorced over your objections. Even more serious, you can be forcibly separated from your children, your home, and your property.
>
> Myth 2: *We cannot force people to remain married and should not try.*
> Fact: It is not a matter of forcing anyone to remain married. The issue is taking responsibility for one's actions in abrogating an agreement. With no-fault divorce, the spouse who

divorces without grounds or otherwise breaks the marriage agreement (for example, by adultery or desertion) thereby incurs no onus of responsibility. Indeed, that spouse gains advantages.

Myth 3: *No-fault divorce has led men to abandon their wives and children.*
Fact: This does happen (wives more often than children), but it is greatly exaggerated. The vast majority of no-fault divorces—especially those involving children—are filed by wives. In fact, as Judy Parejko, author of *Stolen Vows*, has shown, the no-fault revolution was engineered largely by feminist lawyers. Overwhelmingly, it has served to separate large numbers of children from their fathers.

Myth 4: *When couples cannot agree or cooperate about matters like how the children should be raised, a judge must decide according to "the best interest of the child."*
Fact: It is not the business of government officials to supervise the raising of other people's children. The entire point of a marriage and family is for mothers and fathers to cooperate and compromise for the sake of children and provide an example to those children of precisely these principles, without which no family can operate.

Myth 5: *Divorce must be made easy because of domestic violence.*
Fact: Actual physical violence is legitimate grounds for divorce and always has been. So it does not justify dispensing with all standards of justice, which is what no-fault entails. By dispensing with standards of justice for divorce, we have

allowed them to be abandoned for criminal justice too. Thus domestic violence and child abuse are not adjudicated as criminal assault and the accused seldom receives a trial or chance to clear his name. Instead he simply loses his children until he can prove his innocence, an impossible standard.

No-fault divorce has exacerbated the divorce epidemic on almost every count. We urgently need an extensive public debate on divorce and the connected issues of child custody, domestic violence, child abuse, and child support—precisely the debate that the divorce industry has suppressed for four decades.

Other Areas of Support for Marriage

The Catholic Church has long required premarital counseling. Most often, this is done through pre-Cana classes and conferences, part of which includes a premarital inventory—a one-hundred-question survey about everything from money to sex, children, and compatibility. The Church also sponsors marital stability through Marriage Encounter weekends, the Couple-to-Couple League, and marital counseling. All of these groups encourage prayer, regular Church attendance, and active participation in the sacraments as spiritual building blocks for strengthening family life. By and large, this works.

Other religious-sponsored efforts to renew married life include Retrouvaille and Promise Keepers. Retrouvaille, a Catholic program, recruits couples that have weathered their own marital problems to run seminars for other couples in trouble. The participants have been through what most couples experience as the early stages of marriage: romance, casual irritation, and disillusionment. At the third stage, many couples decide to bail out. They don't realize they could work their way back to a stable and happy relationship. At Retrouvaille, couples hear success stories of forgiveness, getting over hurts, and dealing with conflict. Then they are taught how to do this themselves.

Promise Keepers works to motivate fathers to live up to their marriage vows. Rallies are held in stadiums around the country to inspire fathers to be Promise Keepers. These rallies are followed by small group meetings of dads who pray and discuss ways to deepen their marital commitment.

Divorce Has Consequences

In the 1970s, Judith Wallerstein, a psychologist who taught at the University of California, Berkeley, began researching the effects of divorce on children. She continued her research over the next forty years, writing about marriage and divorce right up until her death in 2012, at the age of ninety. Though Wallerstein was not particularly a foe of divorce, believing that separation was a better option than severe marital conflict, she was a strong advocate for how the divorce affected children, and the often unacknowledged consequences.

In a post on the Slate website dated July 13, 2012, Sandra Blakeslee, who coauthored several books with Wallerstein, wrote an article that included this information.

Given her initial idea that divorce may not be so bad, it's ironic that Judy became best known as one of the nation's leading critics of divorce. The heart of her findings:

- The effects of divorce on children are not transient. They are long-lasting and profound, persisting well into adulthood.
- The quality of the post-divorce family is critical. Parents are told "don't fight" but the issue is much bigger. Beyond custody

and visiting plans, children need to be fully supported as they grow up. Few are.

- Age matters. Little ones, ages two to six, are terrified of abandonment. Elementary-school-age children, seven to eleven, grow resentful when deprived of opportunities they would have had if their parents had stayed together. Preadolescents, ages eleven and twelve, can be seduced by what Judy called "the voices of the street." Many teenagers, taking on the role of parent, become overburdened.
- Stepfamilies are laden with land mines that no one sees coming.

Thanks in large part to Judy's work, there is greater attention today to the needs of children after divorce. Lawyers, mediators, judges, educators, counselors, husbands, and wives have heard her message, even if they've never heard her name.

The *Catechism* urges governments and other social groups to help families achieve stability and cohesiveness. "The family must be helped and defended by appropriate social measures. Where families cannot fulfill their responsibilities, other social bodies have the duty of helping them and of supporting the institution of the family" (*CCC*, 2209).

Among the suggestions given to lawmakers is the termination of no-fault divorce and that access to sperm banks be denied to unmarried women. Tax laws should be reexamined to make them marriage friendly and pro-family. Harder to get at, but essential, is to upgrade society's expectation of marriage and family. Expectation affects performance. If the culture turns around and begins to expect couples to stay married and makes their children's needs a priority, then that will happen.

Honor Your Father and Mother

The Catholic family is the domestic Church. Divine love brings the family into existence and calls its members to communion with each other. The bond of love that begins between husband and wife should flow into the broader communion of the family, of parents and children, of brothers and sisters, of relatives and other members of the household. Indeed, the communion of the family is a "sign and image of the communion of Father and Son in the Holy Spirit" (*CCC*, 2205). The family is an image of the Holy Trinity itself.

In plain language, families are where we learn to love and care for one another, especially the most needy: the children, the sick, the elderly. In a loving family, each member is empowered to share joys, sorrows, and talents, to develop oneself fully for service to family, to God, to society.

Parents and children have a unique opportunity to grow closer in love when each gives and receives. When children love, respect, and obey their parents, they make a positive and essential contribution to building a Christian family. In this way children, in turn, activate the gifts of their parents, releasing their energies of love, education, and experience on behalf of the children. A healthy family is a dynamic and life-giving cycle of love.

The *Catechism* points out the importance of honoring our parents throughout life: "Respect for parents derives from gratitude toward those who, by the gift of life, their love and their work, have brought their children into the world and enabled them to grow in stature, wisdom and grace.... Filial respect is shown by true docility and obedience.... The fourth commandment reminds grown children of their responsibilities toward their parents" (*CCC*, 2215, 2216, 2218).

When parental instincts are wedded to Christian faith, the parents identify their calling as a Christian ministry to the welfare of their children. Such parents serve their children well when they call them to responsible freedom. This is in fact a gift from the child to the parent who is offered the remarkable chance to impart the virtues, both human and divine, that will give the child the possibility of a loving adulthood. In this way parents and children honor one another with dignity as human persons and images of God.

Sacrificial love is the hallmark of family relations between spouses as well as those between parents and children. Every family faces the trials of selfishness, anger, tension, quarrels, and competing demands. Parents, brothers, and sisters all must learn together to be open to the healing oil of forgiveness, reconciliation, understanding, generosity of heart, hugs, and kisses that restore the unity of the family.

God calls all families to the joy of renewing themselves with peace and love, especially through the sacraments of reconciliation and Eucharist. These sacraments communicate the graces of the Holy Spirit moving families to overcome every division and to strive for complete communion among themselves.

No Christian family can survive without prayer. Family prayer provides the experience of faith growth, which puts soul into the more explicit faith events of religious education and sacramental celebration. Yes, children must learn their doctrine and acquire the virtue of religion through regular participation in the sacraments. But family prayer is to faith what fresh air and sunshine are to human health. Without family prayer, the seeds of doctrine and sacraments will not fall on sufficiently receptive ground.

Pope John Paul II links family prayer to its celebrations. "Joys and sorrows...births and birthdays, wedding anniversaries... separations and homecomings, important and far-reaching decisions, the deaths of loved ones—all are marks of God's loving interventions in the family's history. They should be seen as teachable moments for thanksgiving...and trusting surrender of the family to God's loving care" (*Christian Family,* 59).

The Family Bill of Rights

The family and society should support one another. In reality this is not always the case. In some cases, governments enact laws that unjustly violate the essential rights of families. There are cultures that fail to serve the family and violently attack family values. The failure of American law to supervise violent media entertainment is one instance.

As the *Catechism* says, "The importance of the family for the life and well-being of society entails a particular responsibility for society to support and strengthen marriage and the family. Civil authority should consider it a grave duty 'to acknowledge the true nature of marriage and the family, to protect and foster them, to safeguard public morality and promote domestic prosperity'" (*CCC,* 2210).

The Synod of Bishops at Rome in 1980 issued a Bill of Rights on behalf of families. Here are some of them:

- the right to exist and progress as a family, that is, the right of every human being, even if he or she is poor, to found a family and to have adequate means to support it
- the right to exercise its responsibility regarding the transmission of life and to educate children

- the right to believe in and profess one's faith and to propagate it;
- the right, especially of the poor and sick, to obtain physical, social, political and economic security
- the right to protect minors by adequate institutions and legislation from harmful drugs, pornography, alcoholism, etc.

The family does not receive its legitimacy from a government: It existed before the state. As Vatican II's *Gaudium et Spes* teaches, the human person is the center and crown of creation. It is in Jesus Christ that the full dignity and potential of a person may be seen and understood (see *Gaudium et Spes*, 12, 22). The family is the best place to nourish and protect this vision.

Growing in Faith

- How has your childhood family experience shaped your outlook on family life?
- How does our culture support families? How does it hurt families?
- What are some practical ways your family can pray together?

Growing in Knowledge

- Why do we call the family the domestic Church?
- What are some ways the Church can help to strengthen family life?
- What does it mean to say the family is an image of the Holy Trinity?

CHAPTER SEVEN

Playing God with Human Life

BECAUSE OF THE IMPORTANCE OF the Fifth Commandment in today's society, I will devote two chapters to its teachings. This chapter will highlight the *Catechism*'s treatment of pro-life concerns in medical-moral matters: abortion, in vitro fertilization, embryo research (stem cell), euthanasia. The next chapter will treat war and the death penalty.

The Fifth Commandment is meant to protect human life even as it speaks against willful murder. Besides terrorism, this commandment also addresses incendiary issues such as abortion, euthanasia (deliberate killing of the aged or infirm), the use of human embryos for medical research, and capital punishment.

Pope John Paul II's encyclical *Evangelium Vitae* (The Gospel of Life) splendidly complements the teaching of the *Catechism* about life and death. The pope contrasts the world's "culture of death" to the Bible's "culture of life." From the story of Cain and Abel, through the prophets and psalms, the pope sees the Hebrew Bible testifying to the God-given gift of life. Killing the innocent denies the human dignity of people born in the image of God. Jesus taught and witnessed the very same message.

"Human life is sacred because from its beginning it involves the creative action of God and it remains forever in a special relationship with the Creator, who is its sole end. God alone is the Lord of life from its beginning to its end: No one can under any circumstances claim for himself the right directly to destroy an innocent human being" (*CCC*, 2258).

Read the above words aloud, slowly. Then think of them in the cultural climate of Europe and America, where life is threatened at its beginning and end by abortion and euthanasia, precisely at the weakest moments in human life. Think also of those who argue that such terminations of life are human rights that should be protected by civil authority and law.

"The inalienable rights of the person must be recognized by civil society and political authority. As a consequence of the respect and protection which must be ensured for the unborn child from the moment of conception, the law must provide appropriate penal sanctions for every deliberate violation of the child's rights" (*CCC*, 2273).

The pope says that politicians cannot separate private conscience from public conduct. In countries where abortion and euthanasia are legal, in the face of being unsuccessful in outlawing these practices, politicians may support laws that at least restrict them. "Society has the right to protect itself against the abuses which can occur in the name of conscience and under the pretext of freedom" (*Gospel of Life*, 71). The pope sees in these developments an "eclipse of conscience." Opponents should resist civil and political approval of abortion and euthanasia with nonviolent and conscientious objection (see *Gospel of Life*, 73).

In Vitro Fertilization

In an article on the Catholic News Agency website titled "In Vitro Fertilization: Why Not?" Rev. Thomas Berg, executive director of the Westchester Institute for Ethics and the Human Person wrote:

> The Catholic Church teaches that IVF is morally illicit without exception, even when the couple uses their own egg and sperm, and without super-ovulation of the mother or the creation of multiple embryos for implantation. Catholics and non-Catholics alike have struggled to understand this moral teaching and wonder how the Church can condemn a medical procedure aimed at bringing about new human lives. The answers lies in even deeper reasons for this moral teaching which reach down into the very core of what it means to be husband and wife.
>
> ...The Church fully supports the endeavors of physicians such as Dr. Thomas Hilgers, director of the Pope Paul VI Institute for the Study of Human Reproduction. His natural methods of overcoming infertility, known as NaPro Technology, have helped hundreds of couples to achieve a pregnancy without recourse to illicit means.

In the words of the *Catechism*, "Since it must be treated from conception as a person, the embryo must be defended in its integrity, cared for, and healed as far as possible, like any other human being. It is immoral to produce human embryos intended for exploitation as disposable biological material" (CCC, 2274–2275).

What then of prenatal diagnosis? "Prenatal diagnosis is morally licit, if it respects the life and integrity of the embryo and the human fetus and is directed toward its safeguarding or healing as an individual. It is gravely opposed to the moral law when this is done with the thought of possibly inducing an abortion, depending upon the results: A diagnosis must not be the equivalent of a death sentence" (*CCC*, 2274).

Some couples become demoralized in their failure to conceive. They may harbor resentment against each other, the Church, and even God. Their feelings are understandable and must be addressed honestly, openly, sensitively. The Church stands with these couples, approving a full range of legitimate choices, including medical treatments that assist, rather than replace the conjugal act, and the option of adoption.

Beyond in vitro fertilization is the field of embryo research, and the Catholic Church rejects such research. On the other hand, a panel at the National Institute of Health (NIH) has recommended federal funding of embryo research. NIH guidelines approve the following types of research: creating embryos solely for research purposes; studies to improve successful pregnancies; research on the process of fertilization; studies on embryonic cells.

Father Tad Pacholcyzk is on the staff of the National Center for Bioethics in Philadelphia. His father was an accomplished scientist, and he is trained in neuroscience. He has conducted a "boot camp" on stem cell issues for the seminarians at St. Charles Seminary in Philly, given numerous speeches, and written many columns on Catholic moral teaching regarding embryo research and IVF. I attended one of his seminars and noted his support for adult stem cell research.

He argued, ironically, that despite all of the media attention that has been devoted to embryonic stem cell research for therapeutic use, the greatest advances in stem-cell research so far have come through adult stem-cell research: Dozens of therapeutic uses have been developed and are currently in use. And the recent discovery of amniotic stem cells may well provide scientists with all the advantages that they had hoped to derive from ESCR, but without any of the moral objections.

Abandon Euthanasia

The *Catechism* says this of euthanasia: "Those whose lives are diminished or weakened deserve special respect. Sick or handicapped persons should be helped to lead lives as normal as possible. Whatever its motives or means, direct euthanasia consists in putting an end to the lives of handicapped, sick, or dying persons. It is morally unacceptable" (*CCC,* 2276–2277).

For the most part, state and federal courts have been ruling against a constitutional right to die. One of the most important rulings in recent years is a decision written by John Noonan of the Ninth Circuit Court. He overruled the May 1994 decision of Judge Barbara Rothstein in Compassion in Dying *v.* Washington State. Judge Noonan cited five special reasons why this is a bad idea, paraphrased as follows:

1. We should not have physicians in the role of killers of their patients. It would perversely affect their self-understanding and reduce their desire to look for cures for disease, if killing instead of curing were an option.
2. We should not subject the elderly and infirm to psychological pressures to consent to their own deaths.
3. We should protect the poor and minorities from exploitation. Pain is a significant factor in the desire for doctor-assisted suicide. The poor and minorities often do not have the resources for alleviation of pain.

4. We should protect all the handicapped from societal indifference and antipathy and any bias against them.
5. We should prevent abuse similar to what has happened in the Netherlands.

The situation in the Netherlands was covered in a book by psychiatrist Herbert Hendin, titled *Seduced by Death: Doctors, Patients, and the Dutch Cure*. A review of the book in *Publishers Weekly*, published shortly after its release, notes:

> Advocates of legalizing assisted suicide and euthanasia for terminally ill or chronically suffering patients often point to the Netherlands as a model, the only Western industrialized country that has embraced these practices. Hendin, a New York City psychiatrist and executive director of the American Suicide Foundation, whose goal is suicide prevention, traveled to Holland to research this important and alarming report. He found that Dutch doctors aggressively market physician-assisted suicide and euthanasia; that mercy killing has become almost a routine way of dealing with serious or terminal illness, even with grief; that the Dutch accept assisted suicide for depressed, suicidal psychotherapy patients who do not respond quickly to treatment; and that many wrongful deaths occur as doctors increasingly exercise paternalistic control over patients....
>
> In the U.S., Hendin believes, legalizing assisted suicide and euthanasia would make large numbers of the poor, minority groups and older people especially vulnerable to pressure by family, physicians, hospitals and nursing homes. As an alternative, he recommends palliative care in a hospice or at home, plus advance directives, a living will, and a health-care

proxy stipulating what you would want done should you become incapable of making decisions.[12]

Catholic opposition to euthanasia does not mean that extraordinary efforts are needed to keep people alive: "Discontinuing medical procedures that are burdensome, dangerous, extraordinary, or disproportionate to the expected outcome can be legitimate. Here one does not will to cause death; one's inability to impede it is merely accepted" (*CCC*, 2278).

Dying patients deserve our care nonetheless. "Even if death is thought imminent, the ordinary care owed to a sick person cannot be legitimately interrupted. The use of painkillers to alleviate the sufferings of the dying, even at the risk of shortening their days, can be morally in conformity with human dignity if death is not willed as either an end or a means, but only foreseen and tolerated as inevitable" (*CCC*, 2279).

In the many agonizing decisions related to death and dying, these general principles must guide us. Pastoral problems and conscience dilemmas will continue to spread as technology advances and new questions arise. As you search for practical answers, I would recommend reading Archbishop Daniel Pilarczyk's *Twelve Tough Issues and More: What the Church Teaches and Why.*

We must celebrate the God of life in our hearts and the gift of eternal life from which all other life proceeds. We are called to care for everyone, especially those who are poorest, most alone, most in need. It is our calling to make the Gospel of Life penetrate the heart of every man and woman and every part of society by proclamation, catechesis, preaching, dialogue, and education. Life and its defense is the duty not only of Christians but also of every person on earth.

Growing in Faith

- Name an experience that taught you life is sacred.
- Why is faith an essential element in pro-life efforts?
- In what ways did Jesus show the importance of each and every human life?

Growing in Knowledge

- Why is human life sacred?
- When is embryo research unethical?
- How can we best treat dying people with love, compassion, care, and affection?
- Name some ways you can help counter the spread of abortion, euthanasia, and embryo research.

CHAPTER EIGHT

The Threat of War and the Search for Peace

> Two bombs struck near the finish line of the Boston Marathon on Monday, turning a celebration into a bloody scene of destruction. Boston Police Commissioner Ed Davis said Monday night that the death toll had risen to three. Scores were injured at the scene. One of the dead was an 8-year-old boy, according to a state law enforcement source. Hospitals reported at least 144 people are being treated, with at least 17 of them in critical condition and 25 in serious condition. At least eight of the patients are children. At least 10 people injured had limbs amputated, according to a terrorism expert briefed on the investigation. "It felt like a huge cannon," a witness told CNN about one of the blasts.[13]

WELCOME TO WHAT SOME PEOPLE call "postmodern war." You see a civilian shot on a city street. Nearby waits a TV cameraman. The grisly scene becomes a video. A United Nations soldier sent to be a peacekeeper watches some terrible act, forbidden to act beyond his mandate. Acts of random terrorism, like the one described above, seem to occur with alarming regularity throughout the world. Here is war where there is no distinction between armies and civilians, where the central authority is ineffective and the ability to end the war through negotiation is very difficult.

Gloomy and depressing as this is, it must not diminish our moral resolve to bring peace to all peoples. Jesus made the search for peace one of his eight beatitudes: "Blessed are the peacemakers, for they will be called children of God" (Matthew 5:9). The Fifth Commandment contains the challenge of peace as well as the condemnation of killing.

The *Catechism* has a strong message about war and peace and the death penalty. In this chapter, we will highlight three challenges that the *Catechism* draws from Catholic teaching

Work actively and consciously for peace.

Mitigate the horrors of war.

Close the death chamber.

We will also look at a few other recent Church teachings that relate to these pro-life issues.

Work for Peace

Pope John XXIII published his most powerful and inspiring encyclical, *Pacem in Terris* (Peace on Earth), on Holy Thursday, April 11, 1963. The world had just pulled back from the brink of nuclear war in the Cuban missile crisis. So appealing was his message that it was printed in full by *The New York Times*. *Time* magazine declared him Man of the Year because of his work for peace.

Pope John's blueprint for peace centered on the need to respect the dignity of the human person. Practically this means defending the rights of all peoples. The pope stated that these rights include what a person needs for basic survival, religious and political freedom, education in culture and technology, the ability to raise a family, work that is both satisfying and properly remunerative, ownership of property, freedom to join associations and unions, and freedom to emigrate and participate actively in the political process.

The state should protect and advance these rights. Without the justice supported by these rights there can be no peace. Pope John quoted St. Augustine on this point: "Take away justice, and what are kingdoms but mighty bands of robbers" (*Pacem in Terris,* 92). Pope John spoke of peace as a free gift, a grace from Christ the Prince of Peace (167). Peace is not attainable by human efforts alone, essential as they are. This stirring call to peace caught the world's imagination partly because it came from someone who had no power in the conventional sense. Its authority arose from what was said and the hope it inspired.

The *Catechism* continues this understanding of peace: "Peace is not merely the absence of war, and it is not limited to maintaining a balance of powers between adversaries. Peace cannot be attained on earth without safeguarding the goods of persons, free communications among [all], respect for the dignity of persons and peoples, and the assiduous practice of fraternity. Peace is the work of justice and the effect of charity" (CCC, 2304).

At our everyday level we can promote peace in a variety of ways. Among these I suggest first that we honor and revere the sacredness of each person we meet as an image of God. Second, I would take Pope John's list of rights and use them as a daily reminder of what we need to do for our neighbor, our community, and our country. This will involve banishing our angers, hatreds, and biases toward others.

The U.S. bishops, in November 1994, issued a pastoral message entitled *Confronting a Culture of Violence: A Catholic Framework for Action*. "Beyond the violence in our streets," they said, "is the violence in our hearts. Hostility, hatred, despair and indifference are at the heart of the growing culture of violence." The U.S. bishops' 1983 peace pastoral speaks of disarming our hearts: "We cannot have peace with hate in our hearts."

Working for peace also means making positive efforts to improve the social conditions of those who need our help. It means active participation in the political process so that the government is responsive to people's basic rights.

The protection of human rights always includes the call to civic and religious duties. Every right has a corresponding duty. If I have a right to a decent education, I also have a duty to be a responsible learner and to help others have the same opportunities I have. During the protests against the Vietnam War, the rallying cry of demonstrators was, "Give peace a chance." This will happen when we are vigilant about justice, love, and mercy for every human being.

Mitigate the Horrors of War

The old saying, "All's fair in love and war," is not Christian teaching. Just because a war has started does not mean the moral law has stopped. Genocide is evil. The indiscriminate destruction of whole cities and their inhabitants is wrong. Wounded soldiers and prisoners of war deserve humane treatment.

In the words of the *Catechism*: "The Church and human reason both assert the permanent validity of the moral law during armed conflict. Noncombatants, wounded soldiers, and prisoners must be respected and treated humanely. Actions deliberately contrary to the law of nations and to its universal principles are crimes, as are the orders that command such actions. Blind obedience does not suffice to excuse those who carry them out. Thus the extermination of a people, nation, or ethnic minority must be condemned as a mortal sin. One is morally bound to resist orders that command genocide" (*CCC*, 2312–2313).

The development of modern scientific weapons—nuclear, biological, and chemical—has vastly increased the destructive potential of today's warfare. This new situation makes one wonder how the Church's teaching on just wars can be applied today. While admitting the legitimate right of self-defense (*CCC*, 2308), the *Catechism* outlines the principles of the just war doctrine as follows:

> The strict conditions for *legitimate defense by military force* require rigorous consideration. The gravity of such a decision makes it subject to rigorous conditions of moral legitimacy. At one and the same time:
>
> —the damage inflicted by the aggressor on the nation or community of nations must be lasting, grave and certain;
>
> —all other means of putting an end to it must have been shown to be impractical or ineffective;
>
> —there must be serious prospects of success;
>
> —the use of arms must not produce evils and disorders graver than the evil to be eliminated. The power of modern means of destruction weighs very heavily in evaluating this condition (*CCC*, 2309, emphasis in original).

In 1983 the Roman Catholic bishops of the United States formally rejected nuclear war:

> Under no circumstances may nuclear weapons or other instruments of mass slaughter be used for the purpose of destroying population centers or other predominantly civilian targets. We do not perceive any situation in which the deliberate initiation of nuclear warfare, on however a restricted scale, can be morally justified. One of the criteria of the just-war tradition is reasonable hope of success in bringing about justice and peace. We must ask whether such a reasonable hope can exist once nuclear weapons have been exchanged. The burden of proof remains on those who assert that meaningful limitation is possible.[14]

Pope Francis underlined his concern about the continuing bloodshed in Syria during a meeting on June 5, 2013, with Catholic charitable groups that are active in the Middle East. Speaking to representatives of relief agencies who had been brought together by the Pontifical Council Cor Unum, the Pope thanked them for their efforts "for the people, often defenseless," who are suffering as a result of the civil war in Syria.

Noting that Pope Benedict XVI had pleaded for a negotiated peace in Syria, and urged humanitarian help for those affected by the fighting, Pope Francis said: "The destiny of the Syrian people is a concern that is also close to my heart."[15]

We should be less worried about justifying a given war and more dedicated to stopping war altogether. In the 1960s, President John F. Kennedy said, "Mankind must put an end to war, or war will put an end to mankind."[16]

We should do all we can to stop the so-called logic of retaliation and revenge. It is better to make room for dialogue and patient waiting, which is more effective than the hasty deadlines of war. On Calvary's cross, without violent resistance, Jesus spoke of forgiveness of enemies and the abolition of revenge. He had preached, "Love your enemies and pray for those who persecute you" (Matthew 5:44).

When he rose from the dead, his first words were about peace: "Peace be with you. As the Father has sent me, so I send you" (John 20:21). Ultimately, peace is a gift from God. Humanly speaking, we must do all we can to achieve it. Divinely speaking, we must never stop imploring God with fervent prayer for this most precious gift of peace.

Capital Punishment

The U.S. Supreme Court halted the death penalty in 1967, ruling that it was implemented arbitrarily and constituted cruel and unusual punishment. That same court reversed its decision in 1976, stating capital punishment can be employed if administered fairly.

A national poll of Roman Catholic adults conducted by Zogby International found that Catholic support for capital punishment has declined dramatically in recent years. The Zogby Poll was released on March 21, 2005, at a press conference of the United States Conference of Catholic Bishops as it announced a new initiative, the Catholic Campaign to End the Use of the Death Penalty.

The poll revealed that only 48 percent of Catholics at that time supported the death penalty. Comparable polls by other organizations had registered 68 percent support among Catholics in

2001. In addition, the percentage of Catholics who are strongly supportive of capital punishment has been halved, from a high of 40 percent to 20 percent in the most recent survey. Statistics published in Fall of 2013 on the Death Penalty Information Center website note, "Only 24% of Catholics—compared to 33% of the general population—supported the death penalty when respondents were given a range of alternative punishments for murder."

Crimes such as the Boston Marathon bombing, the murders at Virginia Tech in 2007, and incidents of terrorism in the wake of the destruction of September 11, 2001, makes our decision about what to do with violent criminals more difficult. The outrage and anger generated by these crimes against humanity makes the call for the death penalty for the guilty parties understandable. But this only fires up the anti-life mindset that has been created by the culture of death. Abortions, euthanasia, and the prevailing violent crime rate all are evidence of moral decay. We will not become more civilized by becoming more barbaric.

The *Catechism* says, "The defense of the common good of society requires that an unjust aggressor be rendered unable to inflict harm. For this reason, those who legitimately hold authority also have the right to use arms to repel aggressors against the civil community entrusted to their responsibility.... Assuming that the guily party's identity and responsibility have been fully determined, the traditional teachg of the Church does not exclude recourse to the death penalty, if this is the only possible way of effectively defending human lives against the unjust aggressor" (CCC, 2265, 2267).

Pope John Paul II addresses the matter in his encyclical *Evangelium Vitae* (The Gospel of Life). "The nature and extent of the punishment must be carefully evaluated and decided upon, and ought not go to the extreme of executing the offender except in cases of absolute necessity: in other words, when it would not be possible otherwise to defend society. Today however, as a result of steady improvements in thepenal system, such cases are very rare, if not practically nonexistent" (The Gospel of Life, 56).

It is clear from this passage that the pope has interpreted the *Catechism*'s teaching about the permissibility of the death penalty in a very restrictive sense. In his view, cases of extreme gravity mentioned by the *Catechism* are now "very rare, if not practically nonexistent." This matter is best seen, not through a legal argument about the death penalty or against the background of danger and revenge, but in the light of building a culture of life.

The life which we possess as human beings and which we have received from God is very different from the life of every other creature. This truth is obscured in our day, which makes us think of ourselves as merely advanced animals. Genesis tells us that humankind is the crowning achievement of God's labors. It clearly teaches the primacy of human life over the rest of creation. Human life is a divine breath that is breathed into us so that we may live.

That is why we are perennially dissatisfied with anything short of God. That is what draws us to one another. We sense in one another the divine spark that attracts us to each other on a deeper level than physical beauty. Disobedience marred God's plan and resulted in our losing sight of the meaning of our lives and true relationship to God and one another. Choosing ourselves in preference to God makes it easy to choose ourselves in preference to everyone else.

The gospel of life is about eternal life, the life offered us through Jesus. Our lives as children of God become the place where God manifests himself. Our lives do not belong to us, but to God our Creator and Father. The highest expression of respect for ourselves and others is the commandment to love one another as we love ourselves (see Leviticus 19:18).

It is through the words, actions, and person of Jesus that we understand the complete truth about the value of human life. All the death issues we have discussed can only be solved by contemplating the life issues centered in Jesus Christ who, as John's Gospel (11:25) says, is our "resurrection and life."

Growing in Faith

- How do you help those in your family appreciate the precious value of human life?
- What is the most challenging pro-life teaching of the Church for you? Why?
- What can you do to promote peace?

Growing in Knowledge

- Why does the Church teach that justice is the best way to assure peace in the world?
- Can there be a just nuclear war? Why or why not?
- What are the Church's arguments against the death penalty?

CHAPTER NINE

God's Plan for Marriage and Sex

EVERY DAY MIRIAM HELPS BOB up the stairs in front of their house atop a steep hill. He still does the driving around town for them, but they are getting on in years. On warm evenings they sit on their porch where they can watch neighbors mow lawns or tend children. Bob waits on Miriam, serving cold lemonade. "We didn't think about getting old when we moved into this house with all its stairs thirty-eight years ago," Miriam says. But they remain there, being together, helping each other with the little things. Somehow just being in each other's presence makes all of life's challenges seem less important. Miriam and Bob, after a lifetime together, love each other.

What is Miriam and Bob's secret to happiness? They've learned and accepted that, over time, the little things add up to make a marriage. At the wedding, lofty promises are made before family and the worshiping community. Newlyweds make plans in decades. But outside of the exciting periods of transition—moving, having children, new jobs, or whatever surprises life holds—most married life happens in the everyday.

It is in that everyday that the Church holds up the ideal of marriage, an ideal with roots in the Sixth and Ninth Commandments ("Neither shall you commit adultery.... Neither shall you covet your neighbor's wife" [Deuteronomy 5:18, 21]). The Church, through the tradition of marriage, holds sacred the means by which most people will achieve holiness.

In this chapter we'll look at three ways society can help promote this ideal:

1. Preserve the inseparable bond of love and procreation.
2. Restore the ideal of chastity in mind, heart, and body.
3. Listen to the call of fidelity.

Love and Procreation Go Together

> A child does not come from outside as something to be added on to the mutual love of the spouses, but springs from the very heart of that mutual giving, as its fruit and fulfillment. So the Church, which "is on the side of life," teaches that..."each and every marriage act remain ordered *per se* to the procreation of human life." "This particular doctrine, expounded on numerous occasions by the Magisterium, is based on the inseparable connection, established by God, which man on his own initiative may not break, between the unitive significance and the procreative significance which are both inherent to the marriage act." (*CCC*, 2366)[17]

In the film *Indecent Proposal* a rich bachelor offers a married woman a million dollars if she will spend one night with him. She persuades her husband that the bargain is worth it: "Well, it's only my body, not my mind or emotions." With her husband's approval, she accepts the proposal. The rest of the story shows how the adultery nearly wrecks the marriage.

The *Catechism* could have saved them the trouble. It reminds us that sex affects the whole person. "Sexuality affects all aspects of the human person in the unity of his body and soul. It especially concerns affectivity, the capacity to love and procreate, and in a more general way the aptitude for forming bonds with others" (CCC, 2332).

In its teaching on marriage, the *Catechism* returns to the biblical story of creation. God created us male and female in his own image. A man is a person and a woman equally so. Man and woman embody the tenderness and power of God with equal dignity, though in different ways. "The union of man and woman in marriage is a way of imitating in the flesh the Creator's generosity and fecundity" (CCC, 2335).

Jesus referred to the creation narratives of Genesis in his teaching about marriage. When confronted with the practice of divorce in his time, he cited the doctrine of creation and applied it to the indissolubility of marriage. "So they are no longer two, but one flesh. Therefore what God has joined together, let no one separate" (Matthew 19:6; cf Genesis 2:24). In his Sermon on the Mount Jesus taught that adultery is wrong and that lust is evil. "Everyone who looks at a woman with lust has already committed adultery with her in his heart" (Matthew 5:28).

The bond between husband and wife is both conjugal and procreative. Conjugal, mutual love is the unitive aspect of marriage. The procreative aspect of marriage concerns the conception, birth, and education of children. The bond between the unitive and procreative may not be broken. Love and babies must go together. Every marital act must be one of love and be open to the transmission of life.

Contemporary methods of Natural Family Planning (NFP) are making it possible for couples to space the births of their children while remaining faithful to the Church's teaching about the inseparable link between the unitive and procreative aspects of marriage. You can find more information about this method on the Catholic bishops' website.[18]

The *Catechism* lists the following acts as offenses against the dignity of marriage: adultery, divorce, incest, sexual abuse of children by adults, polygamy, and living together without benefit of marriage. Cohabitation undermines the dignity of marriage in several ways. It may involve the rejection of marriage as such or reflect the inability of the couple to make a long-term commitment. It speaks of a free union, but what can *union* mean when the partners make no real and lasting commitment to one another?

Beneath the surface of living together outside of marriage lingers the lack of trust. This situation dismisses the dignity of marriage, destroys the very idea of family, and weakens the fidelity that is the true basis of a love relationship. "Carnal union is morally legitimate only when a definitive community of life between a man and a woman has been established" (*CCC*, 2391).

Be Chaste

Chastity means the successful integration of sexuality within the person, thus achieving the inner unity of body and spirit. Sexuality, in which one's "belonging to the bodily and biological world is expressed, becomes personal and truly human when it is integrated into the relationship of one person to another, in the complete and lifelong mutual gift of a man and a woman" (*CCC*, 2337).

The *Catechism* lists the following sins against chastity: lust, masturbation, adultery, fornication, pornography, prostitution, and homosexual acts (2351–2359).

The book of Tobit tells the story of Sarah, whose first seven husbands all died on their wedding night, killed by a demon, the story says. Tobit's son, Tobias, became her eighth husband. He understood that sexuality should be ordered to conjugal and procreative love. Tobias and Sarah abstained from sex in the first week of their marriage. They centered themselves on a prayerful reflection of the true purposes of marriage. Their temporary celibacy saved the life of Tobias and their marriage. Abstinence made their hearts grow fonder of each other.

In our culture, unlike the ancient Hebrews, we have a courting period of abstinence before marriage, when couples begin their journey of love together. This period of abstinence is an important time for couples to lay down a foundation for a lifetime of respectful love.

The *Catechism* quotes St. Ambrose (who lived in the fourth century), comparing chaste lifestyles: "There are three forms of the virtue of chastity. The first is that of the spouses, the second that of widows, and the third that of virgins. We do not praise any one of them to the exclusion of others. This is what makes the richness of the discipline of the Church" (*CCC*, 2349).

Chastity is a gift of the Holy Spirit, not to be confused with celibacy. Marital, conjugal chastity is characterized by faithfulness and a deepening respect and honor for one's spouse. It is a sacred giving of oneself to another, within the covenant of marital love.

All chastity requires training in self-mastery, which enables true human freedom. Either we govern our passions and find inner harmony and peace or we let ourselves be ruled by our emotions and drives and become unhappy. Free people are not slaves of passion.

Temptations to lust arise from within us as well as from the seductions of other people or from obscene films, music, books, plays, pictures, or stories. If I want to remain faithful to my baptismal promises I must use the means to do so. I must know myself, adopt a suitable asceticism, obey God's commandments, practice moral virtues, and be fervent in prayer.

Self-mastery is a demanding, lifelong project. One can never be sure to have won the battle. "The effort required can be more intense in certain periods, such as when the personality is being formed during childhood and adolescence" (*CCC*, 2342). The task is made easier when the culture supports chastity. At the same time, people's success will help change and improve the culture. Chastity is both a grace (a gift from God) and a result of spiritual effort.

In its discussion of homosexuality, the *Catechism* acknowledges the existence of sexual attraction between members of the same sex. It has taken a variety of forms throughout history, and its origin remains largely unexplained. While opposing homosexual acts as intrinsically disordered and against scriptural teaching and natural law, the *Catechism* calls for just treatment of homosexuals.

"They must be accepted with respect, compassion, and sensitivity. Every sign of unjust discrimination in their regard should be avoided" (*CCC*, 2358). Like everyone else, homosexuals are called to chastity and the gift of inner freedom.

Gay Marriage

Let's face it. God is the author of marriage. God created marriage, and it is God who defined the meaning of marriage. "Then the Lord God said, 'It is not good that the man should be alone; I will make him a helper as his partner.'… Therefore a man leaves his father and his mother and clings to his wife, and they become one flesh" (Genesis 2:18, 24).

Jesus affirmed this teaching. The words of Jesus are as true today as when he spoke them to the Pharisees. "Have you not read that the one who made them at the beginning 'made them male and female,' and said, 'For this reason a man shall leave his father and mother and be joined to his wife, and the two shall become one flesh'?" (Matthew 19:4–6).

The current efforts in the United States to redefine marriage—to ignore the natural law and oppose centuries of understanding marriage from a perspective of revelation, reason, and culture—is a wrong and harmful decision. The biggest concern this causes is its effects on the family bonds between a child and his or her mother or father, who are together in marriage for the sake of forming the next generation of the human race.

In a column in the *Catholic New World*, newspaper for the Archdiocese of Chicago, Cardinal Francis George writes:

> Many, unfortunately, now see marriage only as a private, two-person relationship based on love and sexual attraction rather than as a public social institution governing family life. Further, the claim that one is not equal under law is powerful in our society; it makes one a victim. And the claim that one is being demeaned and personally wounded is even more powerful evidence of victimization. Finally, in a post-Freudian culture one should be free to act on every sexual desire, provided there is no coercion in the relationship.... A newly invented civil right cannot be used to destroy a moral good, lest society itself go into decline.
>
> ...If God cannot be part of public life, then the state itself plays God.[19]

Marriage and Promises! Promises!

In Thornton Wilder's play *The Skin of Our Teeth* Mrs. Antrobus tells her husband what she thinks about the marriage promise: "I didn't marry you because you were perfect. I didn't even marry you because I loved you. I married you because you gave me a promise. (Here she takes off her ring and looks at it.) That promise made up for all your faults. And the promise I gave you made up for mine. Two imperfect people got married and it was the promise that made the marriage."

The *Catechism* picks up a similar theme from St. John Chrysostom, Church Father, gifted preacher, and theologian in the fourth century: "St. John Chrysostom suggests that young husbands should say to their wives: I have taken you in my arms and I love you, and I prefer you to my life itself. For the present life is nothing, and my most ardent dream is to spend it with you in such a way that we may be assured of not being separated in the life reserved for us. I place your love above all things, and nothing would be more bitter or painful to me than to be of a different mind from you" (CCC, 2365).

The primary emphasis of the Sixth Commandment is not adultery so much as fidelity to the promises husbands and wives make to each other. That fidelity reflects what the Bible calls covenant. In the Hebrew covenant, marriage was meant to be an earthly mirror of the wedding between God and Israel. God is the faithful spouse who loves Israel with irresistible affection. In the Christian covenant, marriage is meant to give us a visible reflection of Christ's marriage to his Church. Jesus is the faithful spouse who loves the Church so much he was willing to die for her.

Fidelity to the marital promise removes the imagined boundaries of love. More mutual pleasure results from inventive strategies to improve a marital relationship than from the soul-destroying secrecies of extramarital liaisons. Shakespeare spoke of the delights of fidelity in terms of unshakable love. A blessed assurance flows from fidelity, providing everyday, comfortable security to husband and wife. Their response to each other's irrepressible desire for self-worth and dignity is the most tender gift of one spouse to another.

The happiness that comes to a faithful couple often dazes them. The better they are at fidelity, the more they think themselves very lucky indeed. Each day they awaken, they count themselves blessed to see the love in each other's eyes and confirm it with the embrace that brings their hearts together. The passing years make their love seem younger than when it first began. Couples whose experience reveals the creative results of fidelity will be far more able to treat their children with an organic love rather than love as a functional duty.

Adultery and divorce break the promises of fidelity. Some biblical scholars note that the Hebrew word for adultery is similar to the word for idolatry. Since pagan temples in biblical times often employed prostitutes, they were also havens for adultery. To engage in illicit sexual liaisons under the sign of a false god was also to enter into a false relationship with another person. Covenant acts take place in the sight of a living and true God. Unfaithful acts occur under the sign of delusion.

As Archbishop Fulton J. Sheen wrote:

> Fidelity in marriage means much more than abstaining from adultery. All religious ideals are positive, not negative.

> Husband and wife are pledges of eternal love. Their union in the flesh has a grace which prepares them for union with God. The passing of time wears out bodies, but nothing can make a soul vanish or diminish its eternal value. Nothing on earth is stronger than the fidelity of hearts fortified by the Sacrament of Marriage.[20]

The Irish claddagh ring symbolizes the basic picture of fidelity and how to maintain it. It shows hands folded in prayer around a heart of love, beneath a crown of fidelity. Enduring prayer and everlasting love are the secrets of marital fidelity, which is itself the true secret of happiness.

Growing in Faith

- Why do Catholics consider sex to be sacred?
- Name an experience when you felt that human love was connected to God's love?
- The Church needs more examples of saints who were married. What would their characteristics be?
- How can you help people prepare for Christian marriage?

Growing in Knowledge

- How does Christian marriage reflect both the Hebrew and Christian covenants?
- Why do we say that the Sixth Commandment's primary concern is fidelity rather than adultery?
- What lessons do we learn from Genesis 1–3 about marriage?

CHAPTER TEN

Justice and Love for All

I was eyes to the blind, and feet to the lame. I was a father to the needy, and I championed the cause of the stranger. (Job 29:15–16)

Some years ago an assassin was hired to kill Dom Helder Camara, archbishop of Refice and Olinda in northeast Brazil. The executioner came to the door of his simple wooden home and knocked on the door. A very small, frail-looking man opened the door. Speaking with authority, the visitor said he wanted to see Archbishop Camara.

"I am Dom Helder," replied the little man at the door. His image of the archbishop instantly shattered, the assassin stammered, "You are Dom Helder?" "Yes," answered the man known for standing with the poor. "What do you want? Come in. Do you need me for anything?" "No, no," said the assassin, clearly flustered. "I don't want to have anything to do with you. You are not the kind of man one kills."

"Kill? Why would you want to kill?" asked Dom Helder. "Because I was paid to kill you, but I can't kill you," the assassin stammered. "If you are paid, why don't you kill me?" the archbishop reasoned. "I will go to the Lord." "No," said the assassin. "You are with the Lord." And he got up and went away.

This archbishop remains a shining example of Christ's love, a living example of the Seventh and Tenth Commandments: "Neither shall you steal.... Neither shall you desire your neighbor's house, or field, or male or female slave, or ox, or donkey, or anything that belongs to your neighbor" (Deuteronomy 5:19, 21).

Dom Helder Camara was a tireless worker for the Church and for a world that follows Christ's way of justice, love, mercy, and peace. Dom Helder said that the world will be changed and God's will shall be done through the faithful, persistent efforts of small groups of people who "hope against all hope." Dom Helder is a saint of the Seventh and Tenth Commandments, in which God calls all of us to create a just society and a peaceful world. Such a society becomes possible when we respect human dignity and act as just stewards of the goods of the earth. The Church's social teachings help us to reach those goals.

In this chapter, I would like to highlight three messages from the *Catechism* in the area of social teaching:

1. Act as wise and just stewards of humanity's resources.
2. Respect people and their possessions.
3. Appreciate the Church's social teachings.

Be a Good Steward

> In the beginning God entrusted the earth and its resources to the common stewardship of mankind to take care of them, master them by labor and enjoy their fruits. The goods of the earth are destined for the whole human race. The *right to private property* acquired by work or received from others

> by inheritance or gift does not do away with the original gift of the earth to the whole of mankind. (CCC, 2402–2403, emphasis in original)

Ernst Friedrich "Fritz" Schumacher was an internationally influential economic thinker, statistician, and economist in Britain, serving as Chief Economic Advisor to the UK National Coal Board for two decades. His ideas have been popularized in much of the English-speaking world, and he has this to say about the wealth of the west:

> The foundations of peace cannot be laid by universal prosperity, in the modern sense, because such prosperity, if attainable at all, is attainable only by cultivating such drives as greed and envy, which destroy intelligence, happiness, serenity, and thereby the peacefulness of man. It could well be that rich people treasure peace more highly than poor people, but only if they feel utterly secure—and this is a contradiction in terms. Their wealth depends on making inordinately large demands on limited world resources and thus puts them on an unavoidable collision course—not primarily with the poor who are weak and defenseless, but with other rich people. No one is really working for peace unless he is working for the restoration of wisdom.[21]

Schumacher was inspired by Gandhi's vision of helping the poor. He felt strongly that Gandhi had his finger on the pulse of the masses, and thereby believed that all economic policy must make sense in terms of morality and the poor. He interpreted Gandhian economics as people's economics, and explained the difference between economic reasoning based on "people" as against "goods," as is the case with materialistic economic thinking.

The Genesis account of creation communicates both the value of the created world and the dignity of man and woman as images of God. We are called, as images of God, to be stewards of creation. The world is God's farm, and we are the farmers. The Church teaches that the goods of the earth are destined by God to serve the common good. Stewards know this and act responsibly for this goal (for more on this, read Genesis 1:28–29; 2:15).

The prophets of Israel, such as Amos and Isaiah, acted as the conscience of the people. Worship was important, but social concern for the widow, the orphan, and the alien was just as essential. Prophets taught that the quality of one's faith was tested by the quality of justice in the nation. Justice is stewardship in action. A measure of people's faith was their just treatment of one another—especially the most vulnerable in society. This prophetic message is as important for today as it was in the tenth century B.C.

Jesus continued and enlarged the teachings of Genesis and the prophets. Jesus perfectly embodied what it meant to be an image of God (see Colossians 1:13) and an ideal steward of the earth's goods. Of his many rich teachings, his "sheep and goats talk" best reflects the prophetic concern for the marginalized, the hungry, thirsty, naked, prisoners, the sick, the unjustly treated (Matthew 25:31–40).

Like the prophets, Jesus turns our attention to the widow, orphan, and alien, those at the edge of the circle. He challenges us to care for needy single mothers, illegitimate children, the vast army of refugees, the homeless, and others who need our love. The goods of the earth are not just for us and our families, but for all humanity.

Jeffrey Sachs is an innovative economist, professor at Columbia University, and director of The Earth Institute, an organization of over 850 university professors in science disciplines who support sustainable development. Over his career, he has help Eastern European nations transition from communism to a market economy and has applied his economic theories into real life, in projects such as The Millennium Villages Project, a partnership with the United Nations that operates in ten African countries and covers more than five hundred thousand people, teaching them practices of sustainable development.

Sachs's remarks commemorating the fiftieth anniversary of the March on Washington, a landmark civil rights protest, were noted in the Huffington Post:

> If the arc of the moral universe bends towards justice, as Martin Luther King Jr. reminded us, it is because righteous souls in each generation pull that arc towards its hallowed end. 50 years ago at this spot, King spoke to righteous men and women who braved police dogs and water cannon to fulfill their role in shaping the moral universe. They did their job bravely and well and we honor them today.
>
> Yet the great task of moral construction is never finished. There is no final victory on Earth, only an inheritance of justice that each generation must renew and pass to the next....
>
> It was the genius of the generation of 1963 to recognize the indivisibility of morality. Martin Luther King Jr., John F. Kennedy, and Pope John XXIII knew that racism, poverty, and militarism all carry us away from human needs and aspirations.

> It is our turn to bend the arc of the moral universe. We too must banish the moneylenders, not from the temple but from the lobbies of Congress and the White House. We too must beat swords into plowshares, joining together with Iranians, Egyptians, Palestinians and Israelis, to honor the prophets of peace....
>
> In our age of greed and glitter, the work of justice often seems to be stilled. But do not be deceived. For the ancient cry still moves us today: Justice, justice shall you pursue, so that you may live in the Promised Land.[22]

Respect People and Their Possessions

Armed robbery, from simple street muggings to holdups at ATMs, remains the most prevalent crime that Americans should fear from strangers. Most robberies are committed by strangers, often resulting in serious injury and lost property. Beyond these instances of stealing is the alarming growth of identity theft, Internet scams, white collar crime, fraud, embezzlement, and so on.

Stewardship also involves respect for persons and their possessions. "In economic matters," says the *Catechism*, "respect for human dignity requires the practice of the virtue of *temperance*, so as to moderate attachment to this world's goods; the practice of the virtue of *justice*, to preserve our neighbor's rightsand the practice of *solidarity*, in accordance with the golden rule" (CCC, 2407; emphasis in original).

People are worried about their safety and the security of their possessions. They want stronger police protection and bigger jails for the offenders. They wire their homes with alarms, move into gated communities, and even hire bodyguards.

Over the past fifteen years there has been a movement toward moral and character education in our schools and churches. This is a form of preventive medicine that can certainly help raise a generation of young people who would internalize the virtues of honesty and respect for persons and property.

The *Catechism* advocates the excellent virtues of temperance, justice, and solidarity. Temperance restrains our inclination to greed. Justice teaches us proper regard for the rights of others and their property. Solidarity with all humans instructs us in the beauty of the golden rule, "Do unto others as you would have them do unto you."

Armed with these virtues, we can better appreciate why theft is wrong. It is the usurping of another's property against the reasonable will of the owner. Included under that definition are fraud, paying unjust wages, and forcing prices up by taking unfair advantage of another.

The *Catechism* offers a stewardship list, not meant to be exhaustive, but indicative of failures in responsible stewardship as well as loss of respect for persons and their possessions: "work poorly done, tax evasion, forgery of checks and invoices; excessive expenses and waste. Willfully damaging private or public property is contrary to the moral law and requires reparation" (CCC, 2409).

Good stewards of creation will never engage in enterprises that enslave human beings for any reason whatsoever, be that commercial, political, ideological, or totalitarian. It is a sin against dignity to treat people as merchandise.

Appreciate the Church's Teachings

Social teaching in the Church embraces both Catholic social tradition and an explicit Catholic social doctrine. The social tradition has been part of Church life since her beginning and includes the inheritance of the social consciousness embodied by Genesis, the prophets, and the social concern of the people of God of the Hebrew covenant. Social doctrine refers to the teachings of the popes, councils, and bishops dating from Pope Leo XIII's *Rerum Novarum* in 1891 to the present day.

As the *Catechism* says, "The social doctrine of the Church developed in the nineteenth century when the Gospel encountered modern industrial society with its new structures for the production of consumer goods, its new concept of society, the state and authority, and its new forms of labor and ownership. The development of the doctrine of the Church on economic and social matters attests the permanent value of the Church's teaching at the same time as it attests the true meaning of her Tradition, always living and active" (*CCC*, 2421).

The *Catechism* contains several treatments of the Church's social doctrine in different sections. Read 355–421 for the *Catechism*'s understanding of what it means to be a human being, the origin of human dignity, the problem of the Fall, and the promise of redemption. In the simplest of terms, we learn that we are radically flawed by original and actual sin—and radically redeemed by Christ's saving death and resurrection.

Next look at 1897–1948, where the *Catechism* deals with our participation in social life, the role of authority, the importance of the common good, social justice, and human solidarity. Finally, read 2401–2449, the *Catechism*'s treatment of the Seventh Commandment, most of which pertains to the Church's social doctrine.

To live the Church's social doctrine demands of us the humility and love for the poor exemplified by Mother Teresa whose personal witness influenced Malcolm Muggeridge, an English journalist, author, media personality, and satirist, to become a Catholic at the age of seventy-nine. A post on the website *Fellowship of the Mind*, titled "Coming Home: The Conversion of Malcolm Muggeridge," recalls Muggeridge's meeting with Mother Teresa in 1970, while filming a documentary for the BBC:

> Well, on that fated morning of their meeting (a morning that would change him for the rest of his life) he met her as she was working out in the streets with sick and poor people in a ghetto like he had never seen before, amid stench, filth, garbage, disease, and poverty that was just unbelievable. But what struck Muggeridge more than anything else, even there in that awful squalor and decadence, was the deep, warm glow on Mother Teresa's face and the deep, warm love in her eyes.
>
> "Do you do this every day?" he began his interview.
>
> "Oh, yes," she replied, "it is my mission. It is how I serve and love my Lord."
>
> "How long have you been doing this? How many months?"
>
> "Months?" said Mother Teresa. "Not months, but years. Maybe eighteen years."
>
> "Eighteen years!" exclaimed Muggeridge. "You've been working here in these streets for eighteen years?"
>
> "Yes," she said simply and yet joyfully. "It is my privilege to be here. These are my people. These are the ones my Lord has given me to love."

> "Do you ever get tired? Do you ever feel like quitting and letting someone else take over your ministry? After all, you are beginning to get older."
>
> "Oh, no," she replied, "this is where the Lord wants me, and this is where I am happy to be. I feel young when I am here. The Lord is so good to me. How privileged I am to serve him."
>
> Later, Malcolm Muggeridge said, "I will never forget that little lady as long as I live. The face, the glow, the eyes, the love—it was all so pure and so beautiful. I shall never forget it. It was like being in the presence of an angel. It changed my life. I have not been the same person since. It is more than I can describe."

The service of the poor is a key tenet of all true Christian faith: "Those who are oppressed by poverty are the object of *a preferential love* on the part of the Church which, since her origin and in spite of the many failings of her members, has not ceased to work for their relief, defense and liberation through numerous works of charity which remain indispensable always and everywhere" (*CCC*, 2448; emphasis in original).

When St. Rose of Lima's mother reproached her for caring for the sick and poor at home, Rose said to her: "When we serve the poor and the sick, we serve Jesus. We must not fail to help our neighbors, because in them we serve Jesus." On his deathbed, St. Vincent de Paul was asked of the best way to deal with the poor. "You must love them, sister. Then they will be able to forgive you for the bread you give them."

In his homily on the parable of Lazarus and the Rich Man, St. John Chrysostom said this about ministry to the poor: "Not to enable the poor to share in our goods is to steal from them and deprive them of life. The goods we possess are theirs, not ours." Jesus teaches us, "Whoever has two coats must share with anyone who has none; and whoever has food must do likewise" (Luke 3:11). St. James reinforces this truth, "If a brother or sister is naked and lacks daily food, and one of you says to them, 'Go in peace; keep warm and eat your fill,' and yet you do not supply their bodily needs, what is the good of that?" (James 2:15–16).

Acts of real love for the poor are the best way to start living the Church's social teachings. There is no substitute for personal contact. We are called to heal the symptoms of poverty and injustice. A loving ministry to the poor, the hungry, the naked, the vulnerable, and marginalized is the best way to fulfill this vocation.

We are also called to heal the causes of injustice and poverty. This summons us to examine how business, government, education, medicine, and other social forces affect the helpless in our society and in the poor countries of the world. This is a more complicated task and demands our working together with like-minded people in a common cause.

Solutions are not easy and never swift, but that should only challenge us all the more. We need to be convinced that justice, mercy, and love are possible for all human beings. We must combine our human ingenuity with a reliance on the grace of God to effect a conversion of mind and heart in institutions and leaders. They can join us in bringing the fruits of the kingdom of God into our world.

Luckily, we have an abundant supply of Scripture and Church teachings to guide us. What we need is an army of Christian witnesses, working together with all people of goodwill to accomplish the ideals of justice and love for every person on earth.

Growing in Faith

- Name some Scripture passages that show the attitude of Jesus to the poor.
- People say the Church should stay out of politics. Do you agree or disagree? Why?
- Who inspires you most to love the poor? Why?
- Do you think the poor are treated unfairly? Why or why not?

Growing in Knowledge

- Read Genesis 1:28–29; 2:15. What does this passage say about stewardship?
- Name some positive ways to be good stewards.
- Name a practical way that you can reach out to someone in need.

CHAPTER ELEVEN

Being Truthful—and Free!

WE PROCLAIM THE IDEAL OF telling the truth: "I swear to tell the truth, the whole truth, and nothing but the truth." We talk of truth in lending, truth in advertising, truth in relationships. But we are not strangers to deception and lying. Deep down we realize the truth is often lacking. We believe our personal lives and our society would be better and happier if we lived in the truth. To be truthful is the Eighth Commandment: "Neither shall you bear false witness against your neighbor" (Deuteronomy 5:20). Jesus reveals for us the deepest meaning of that commandment: "And you will know the truth, and the truth will make you free" (John 8:32).

There is an African legend about the eternal struggle between truth and falsehood. In the legend, Truth, Falsehood, Fire, and Water, traveling through the countryside, come upon an abandoned herd of cattle. They agree to divide it up among themselves, but Falsehood plots to get the whole herd. Falsehood tricks Water and Fire out of their share. But Truth will not back down. Truth and Falsehood struggle fiercely, shaking the earth with thunderclaps. But neither can prevail.

Eventually, they call upon Wind to settle their contest. "I cannot judge a winner here," says the wise Wind. Truth and Falsehood are destined to struggle. One time Truth will win; another time, Falsehood. But Truth must always recover, get up again, and fight.

Honesty and truthful living are the bedrock of society. People cannot live together if no one is able to believe what anyone else is saying. God has put into all human beings the drive to seek and expect the truth, and to respond to the challenges that truth demands.

In the Eighth Commandment God calls us to be committed to truthful living, to resist all temptations to deceit, and to open ourselves to the joy and beauty of reality. The *Catechism of the Catholic Church* offers us a framework for responding to God's call to tell the truth and battle falsehood:

1. Live the truth.
2. Remove all deceit from your life.
3. Let truth open you to the joy and beauty of reality.

Live the Truth

The *Catechism* instructs us that we are called to be sincere and truthful: "The disciple of Christ consents to 'live in the truth,' that is, in the simplicity of a life in conformity with the Lord's example, abiding in his truth" (CCC, 2470).

History is full of stories of people who valued the truth so highly they were willing to die for it. St. John Fisher surrendered his life rather than approve of King Henry VIII's divorce or deny the truth that the pope is Christ's appointed head of the Church. Franz Jagerstatter refused to accept the Nazis' big lie and was martyred for his commitment to the truth of Christ. During the French Revolution a convent of Carmelite nuns bravely went to death at the guillotine rather than bow before the goddess of reason or abandon the truth for which their vows stood.

In the trial of Jesus before Pilate, it is clear how central the matter of truth is. When Jesus heard the lies his enemies were telling about him, he responded, "For this I was born, and for this I came into the world, to testify to the truth" (John 18:37). Scripture remembers that the serpent lied to Adam and Eve, which caused them to disobey God and be expelled from Eden. In the presence of Pilate, Jesus—the new Adam—stands for the most important of all truths: that humans need to be saved from sin by God.

Truthful living, therefore, not only makes us people of integrity; by God's grace it transforms us into a saved people. Just as lies make a hell for people on earth, so does living in the truth afford us glimpses of heaven and prepare us for eternal life.

Pilate's skeptical question, "What is truth?" broods like a cloud over modern society. Today's skepticism flattens all statements into opinions. "That's only what you think," we say in an argument. We ignore objective facts. Yet when everyone's truth is accepted, there is a vacuum, a loss of confidence that we can know any truth larger than individual experience and opinion. Self-destructive people will take over where the truth-tellers are silent.

To live in truth, as Jesus urges, demands study, love, and practice. Study alone is not enough, for then truth remains abstract; its full meaning is not grasped. Truth must move to the heart and to behavior before its genuine potential is appreciated. Logical acceptance of truth is only a third of the story. We must also love the truth. The heart must engage truth every bit as much as the mind. Why? Because truth is more than simply an idea.

Truth contains beauty, attractiveness, and the unifying power of love. The mind sees truth as an idea. Love beholds truth as a revelation of beauty, ultimately a revelation of God. Why else would Jesus have said that he not only possessed the truth, but was indeed the living revelation of truth?

Last, truth demands action. This is the triad of truth: to know, to love, to act. Once truth is known, loved, and lived, then its magnificent promise is realized. One of the main reasons why skepticism and relativism have prevailed in our culture is that people think of truth only as an idea divorced from the loving and living—the nitty-gritty of life. When this happens, truth, held only as an idea, withers before the onslaught of the marketplace of ideas where opinions count more than truth.

The positive side of the Eighth Commandment is to live the truth—free from illusions, falsehoods, denials—to face and accept ourselves without pretense or putting ourselves down, to live in reality. The Church insists that truth is more than correct thoughts; it is the object of our love and passion. It is the dynamic motivation for our behavior.

Get Rid of Deceit

In his story *Gulliver's Travels*, satirist Jonathan Swift asked the question, "Why would anyone be dishonest?" He has Gulliver meet a group of people who were so rational they found deceit beyond comprehension. One of them explains to Gulliver, "The use of speech was to make us understand one another and to receive information and facts. Now if anyone said the thing that was not [lies], these ends were defeated."

They believed that lies would have no place in a world that was inhabited by totally reasonable people. We know, however, that we are not totally or merely rational. We wrestle with passions, impulses, drives, and tendencies that do not easily harmonize with reason. To acquire the virtue of truthfulness, we need grace, prayer, study, love and lots of practice!

The *Catechism* says we should be guided by the Golden Rule in revealing information and should respect the privacy of others. We do not have to tell all to the nosy or curious. "The good and safety of others, respect for privacy, and the common good are sufficient reasons for being silent about what ought not be known or for making use of a discreet language" (CCC, 2489).

Physicians, lawyers, and others are bound by professional secrecy, "save in exceptional cases where keeping the secret is bound to cause very grave harm to the one who confided it, to the one who received it or to a third party, and where the very grave harm can be avoided only by divulging the truth" (CCC, 2491).What is told a priest in the sacrament of reconciliation is a special category and cannot be revealed "under any pretext" (CCC, 2490).

Yet lying is a different matter. "Lying is the most direct offense against the truth. To lie is to speak or act against the truth in order to lead someone into error " (CCC, 2483). Lies misuse God's gift of speech, said St. Augustine.

All lies have one thing in common: the intention to mislead, to conceal, to falsify. Lies may confuse the hearers, but liars know exactly what they are doing. It is not always easy to detect a lie. Matters would be simpler if liars' noses grew longer as Pinocchio's did each time he told a lie. Lies come in many shapes and forms. Mark Twain, not entirely in jest, claimed there were 869 forms of lying.

The *Catechism* lists the following types of behavior as reprehensible forms of lying: false witness, perjury, rash judgment, detraction, calumny (false, damaging accusations), destroying the reputation of others, and flattery or encouragement that confirms another in malicious or perverse conduct. (*CCC*, 2475–2481) In all these cases there is lying with the intention to cause harm to others.

Lying not only hurts other people, it also corrupts the one who lies by undermining the trust that is the basis of a wholesome society. Sad to say, one example comes in the form of lawsuits filed against our dioceses concerning the priest abuse scandals. News stories about these incidents frequently feature evidence of untruths on the part of more than one party to the suit.

The mass media, which has acquired such enormous influence in the shaping of public opinion and communicating information, should remember its responsibilities of justice, charity and truth, says the *Catechism*: "By the very nature of their profession, journalists have an obligation to serve the truth, and not offend against charity in disseminating information" (*CCC*, 2497).

As users and consumers of the mass media, we cannot be passive; we need to be alert and actively engaged in searching for the truth. We should be vigilant about the messages and values directed to our children. This means we must form enlightened consciences so that we can more easily resist unwholesome influences upon ourselves and our families.

Each of us must be convinced that truth works better than lies for the health of the family and society. Journalists and entertainers who get beyond the urge to shock, scandalize, and exploit the base appeal of sex and violence will find they make their greatest contribution to society by simply telling the truth in a wise and prudent manner. The more government leaders, by their truthfulness, earn people's trust, the better they are able to lead. Business leaders who want an enthusiastic work force have much more going for them when they are honest and open with their employees. Spouses build trust and show genuine love by being truthful with each other.

Truth works better than lies because it corresponds to the drive that God put in our human natures for happiness and self-realization. Truth brings about the kingdom of love. Deceit releases self-destructive impulses. Truth really does make us free. The more people practice truthful living, the greater is their inner sense of liberation. This is not achieved easily or quickly. The process of truthful living demands a lifetime of struggle and moral courage. A remarkable sense of inner freedom testifies to us that truthful living is its own reward.

Let Truth Bring You Joy

In its final section on the Eighth Commandment, the *Catechism* expounds an inspiring connection between truth and beauty, in both its natural and divine forms. There is a link between truth and art, between truth and the contemplation of the beauty of God. As images of God, we are able to know the truth, desire goodness, and form a community of love with one another.

In the words of the *Catechism*, "The practice of goodness is accompanied by spontaneous spiritual joy and moral beauty. Likewise, truth carries with it the joy and splendor of spiritual beauty. Truth is beautiful in itself. But truth can find other complementary forms of human expression, above all when it is a matter of evoking what is beyond words: the depths of the human heart, the exaltations of the soul, the mystery of God" (CCC, 2500).

But being God's images also includes expressing the truth of this relationship in works of art. The ability to create a work of art in music, poetry, dance, sculpture, painting, architecture, drama, opera, and other forms is a uniquely human act. Beyond our daily work load, our efforts to provide for our families and their future, we have the capacity to create and appreciate art and beauty, the extraordinary flowering of our inner riches.

Art emerges from a talent given by God and is developed by human effort, training, discipline, and lengthy dedication. True art reveals the truth of God and life through a wide range of expression that appeals to our intuition and ministers to our hunger for beauty. "The fine arts, but above all sacred art, 'of their nature are directed toward expressing in some way the infinite beauty of God in works made by human hands. Their dedication to the increase of God's praise and of his glory is more complete, the more exclusively they are devoted to turning men's minds devoutly toward God'" (*CCC*, 2513).[23] True sacred art draws us to adore and love God.

It is the gift of wisdom that inspires this quest for beauty. This quest moves us, also, into a contemplative place where our prayer and appreciation of the wonder of God can come together. Both artists and contemplatives are opened to the truth of God through the emanation of wisdom. "[Wisdom] is a breath of the power of God; and a pure emanation of the glory of the Almighty; For she is the reflection of eternal light, a spotless mirror of the working of God, and an image of his goodness. [I] became enamored of her beauty" (Wisdom 7:25–26; 8:2).

Religion and art have generally been mutually useful to one another. Countless artists have used their talents to reveal the beauty of God to the world. Sacred art—and its visible results in cathedrals and monasteries and parish churches—contains thousands of examples of how truth as God's wisdom has nurtured faith through the centuries. Let us drink at the fountain of truth in all its blessed forms.

Growing in Faith

- How do you feel when you have been deceived? How does this help you avoid deceiving others?
- Who is the most honest person you know? What are you learning from this model of truthfulness?
- How can truth open a person to beauty and joy?

Growing in Knowledge

- What can you do to increase trust among your family, your circle of friends, and your local community?
- What should be done to influence government and the mass media to be more committed to truth and trust building?
- Can you name a time when you told the truth under difficult circumstances?

CHAPTER TWELVE

Virtues: Expressions of God's Image

Osceola McCarty spent a lifetime making other people look nice. For most of her eighty-seven years, she took in bundles of dirty clothes and made them neat and clean for parties she never attended, weddings to which she was never invited, and graduations she never saw.

As a poor black child in Hattiesburg, Mississippi, she had to quit school in the sixth grade to go to work. She never married, never had children, and never learned to drive. She spent very little on herself. She cut the toes out of her shoes to make them fit and bound her ragged Bible with Scotch tape to keep Corinthians from falling out.

Over the years, she saved the dollars and change she earned until it amounted to $150,000. Just before her death she gave it away to the University of Southern Mississippi so that poor black women could get a college education. "I wanted to share my wealth with the children," she said. Business leaders were so inspired by her generosity that they agreed to raise $150,000 to match her gift.

Stephanie Bullock was the first to receive a grant from McCarty's scholarship fund. "It was a miracle and an honor," said Stephanie. She visited McCarty to thank her personally and visited her frequently during the last years of her life, filling a space in McCarty's life that had been empty for decades.

McCarty didn't want a building or statue in her honor. She only wanted one thing: to attend the graduation of a student who made it through college because of her—which she did. Oseola's story is a lovely reminder of how living a Christian moral life can create a beautiful person.

Our study of Part 3 of the *Catechism of the Catholic Church*, dealing with Christian morality, has had much the same goal in mind. At the beginning of this book, we set out some of the *Catechism*'s fundamental moral teachings. In the first three chapters, we explored the primary importance of God's saving grace, the assuring moral guidance of the Church as mother and teacher, the reality of sin, and the benefits of examining our consciences.

In subsequent chapters we have examined the Ten Commandments in the light of the Great Commandment: Christ's call for us to love God, others, and ourselves. In this final chapter we celebrate the gift of being created images of God. I'll present two paths to virtuous living that help us to become the beautiful persons intended by Christ's moral teachings:

1. Discover and respect your true self.
2. Practice the virtues.

Our True Self Is God's Image

The dignity of human persons is rooted in their "creation in the image and likeness of God. Endowed with a spiritual soul, with intellect and free will, the human person is from his [or her] very conception ordered to God and destined for eternal beatitude" (CCC, 1700, 1711).

Shakespeare says, "This above all, to thine own self be true. Then it shall follow, as the day the sun, you can never be false to any man." (*Hamlet*, Act 1, Scene 3.). The search for the real self is always a spiritual and moral quest. The present interest in self-esteem, self-worth, and personal dignity is a contemporary expression of the age-old desire for self-discovery and life's nobility.

The *Catechism* relates the moral life to our divinely given identity as images of God. How can we tell we are images of God? There are five ways.

We can know the truth. Just as God can know and understand people and the world, so God has given us minds that possess the ability to know: "The human person participates in the light and power of the divine Spirit." By reason we are "capable of understanding the order of things established by the Creator" (*CCC*, 1704).

We can love God and others, and choose the good. After shot-down U.S. Air Force pilot Captain Scott O'Grady was rescued in the Balkans during the Serbian war, he said at a press conference, "The first thing I want to do is thank God. If it wasn't for God's love for me and my love for God, I wouldn't have gotten through it. He's the one who delivered me here, and I know that in my heart."

Scripture records many names for God, but none surpasses St. John's compelling teaching that "God is love" (1 John 4:16). God has given us hearts to love and choose the good, and therein lies the secret of happiness. For this reason, the *Catechism* places its teaching on the beatitudes immediately after its consideration of ourselves as images of God. "The beatitudes respond to our natural desire for happiness. This desire is of divine origin: God has placed it in the human heart in order to draw man to the One who alone can fulfill it" (*CCC*, 1718). The eight beatitudes both show us ways to be happy and are motivations for leading the moral life that brings us the joy we desire.

We can act freely in reference to truth and goodness. God always acts freely and has given us the privilege of freedom. Jesus says we are free to do what we should. Our culture tells us we are free to do what we want. It presents us with the false dilemma: Should I conform to moral laws and principles? Or should I be free? The answer is not either/or, but both/and. A ballet dancer gracefully moves about the stage because she or he is disciplined to the laws and principles of ballet.

Shall I be faithful to principles or only to persons? Which makes me free? The answer is both: I should be faithful to persons by means of principles. The path to freedom from sin is through obedience to divine law. To seek freedom without conformity to moral principles is self-destructive. To use the road map of Christ's two laws of love and the Ten Commandments given to Moses is the real highway to freedom.

We discover our greatness comes from God. The film *Chariots of Fire* is about two British runners who became unlikely winners in the 1924 Olympics. One of the heroes, Eric Liddell, is a fervent Scottish Protestant, who plans to be a missionary to China after the games are over. Uncompromising about his moral principles, he forfeits his chance for a major trophy because the trial heat for his race would take place on Sunday. His fidelity to sabbath observance made this a matter of conscience. Through the intervention of one of his rivals, he is entered into another race on a weekday and he wins.

Eric is just as forthright about his belief that his gifts and his greatness come from God. Speaking to his sister, who opposes his running, he says, "I must run. God made me fast." When asked how he could compete so well, he said, "The power is within." At a small dinner with his missionary friends, he confessed, "When I run, I feel God's pleasure."

Eric's story clearly shows us one way in which a believer experienced himself as loved, esteemed and worthwhile because he is an image of God. The supreme source of our personal dignity is God, who has graced us as images of his grandeur.

Chariots of Fire was unlike any other film being made at the time: a story of loyalty, determination, and standing up for what you believe in, refusing to be knocked down when everyone around you wants you to fail.

We reflect the goodness of God by caring for our community. Father Jim Di Perri of Boston was a community activist since his high school days. When Logan Airport was planning a new runway that would send airplanes and their noise over his parish area in Quincy and Squantum, he organized a protest, saying, "I have always admired priests who are civic minded. If a priest does not know how to care for the earthly interests of people, how will he be devoted to their heavenly ones?"

This exemplifies the fifth trait of being an image of God, namely, being community minded. Our faith tells us that God is Trinity, a communion of loving persons. As images of this communal God, we are expected to have a community consciousness and take action when needed.

Being images of God establishes a basic building block of morality. We can know truth, love God, others and self, act freely in truth and goodness with community awareness, and acknowledge our greatness comes from God.

Practice the Virtues

Our purpose in studying Part 3 of the *Catechism* has been both spiritual and moral. Spiritually, our purpose is to deepen our friendship with God and advance toward our final goal, which is heaven. Morally, we strive to acquire the virtues which help us love God, others, and ourselves ever more deeply. We live out our calling as images of God by practicing these virtues.

In the words of the *Catechism*, "The human virtues are stable dispositions of the intellect and will that govern our acts, order our passions, and guide our conduct in accordance with reason and faith. They can be grouped around the four cardinal virtues: prudence, justice, fortitude, and temperance. The theological virtues dispose Christians to live in a relationship with the Holy Trinity.... There are three theological virtues: faith, hope, and charity" (*CCC*, 1834, 1840, 1841).

Back in 1992 a group of educators and philosophers met in the mountains of Colorado and produced something they called the Aspen Declaration. It listed six core elements of character that should be inculcated by families, schools, and other institutions that deal with young people. These virtues are: trustworthiness (including honesty and loyalty), respect, responsibility (including self-discipline and hard work), fairness, caring (compassion), and citizenship (including obeying laws, staying informed and voting).

The current revival of interest in virtues comes at a time when thoughtful people are worried about the fraying of our social fabric, the breakup of too many families, the loss of trust, and the dangerous increase in violence. Throughout its long history, virtue has meant doing the right thing. A virtue is a quality of human character by which individuals habitually recognize and do what is right.

How do children learn virtues? First, by hearing stories of heroes, heroines, and saints that inspire them to imitate their virtuous behavior. All older cultures took it for granted that the young needed to hear stories about ideal behavior. In the nineteenth century, every American public school had McGuffey readers, books that were filled with "stories with a moral," all instilling an array of desired virtues. Traditionally, Catholic school religion texts have presented the virtuous example of Jesus and the lives of other biblical people as well as saints and other admirable figures of Church history.

Character education was once assumed. For a variety of reasons, this ideal has been lost in many of the advanced industrialized societies. But the hunger for it never died. Renewed interest in it proves how durable and desirable the life of virtue is.

The presence and power of the Holy Spirit and the vital action of divine grace are a tremendous help in becoming a virtuous person. The *Catechism* teaches that we need virtues to be moral and we need the Holy Spirit's grace-laden presence to become virtuous. If God, the divine artist, fashioned each of us into a masterpiece image of divinity, how much more does God love and enjoy putting the finishing touches on our lives by the graces he gives us for growing in the virtues.

The *Catechism* lists and explains the traditional virtues. "Prudence disposes the practical reason to discern, in every circumstance, our true good and to choose the right means for achieving it. Justice consists in the firm and constant will to give

God and neighbor their due. Fortitude ensures firmness in difficulties and constancy in the pursuit of good. Temperance moderates the attraction of the pleasures of the senses and provides balance in the use of created goods.... There are three theological virtues: faith, hope and charity" (*CCC*, 1835–1838, 1841). The theological virtues of faith, hope and charity "have God for their origin, their motive and their object" (*CCC*, 1840).

With these all-too-brief thoughts about virtues and our gift as images of God, I conclude this book on the moral teachings found in the *Catechism of the Catholic Church*. I began this book with grace, and let us end with grace. Dorothy Day once said, "I am sure that God did not intend that there be so many poor. The class structure is of our own making and our consent, not His. It is the way we have arranged it and it is up to us to change it."[24]

The humbler we can be on our journey to God, the more we will realize how much his grace means to us. It helps us do the right thing and finally realize: God alone satisfies.

Growing in Faith

- Describe how you are an image of God.
- Which virtues are your strong point?
- Which virtues of Jesus inspire you most?

Growing in Knowledge

- What is a virtue?
- What are the seven traditional virtues?
- Practically speaking, how do we develop virtues?

NOTES

1. Pascal's Wager.
2. James Q. Wilson, *The Moral Sense* (New York: Free Press, 1993).
3. Wilson, *The Moral Sense.*
4. From Teresa's "Maxims."
5. *Treatise on the Love of God.*
6. Alfred McBride, *How to Pray Like Jesus and the Saints: A Study Guide for Catholics* (Huntington, Ind.: Our Sunday Visitor, 2009).
7. Emerging Models of Pastoral Leadership Project and the Center for Applied Research in the Apostolate, 2011, "The Changing Face of U.S. Catholic Parishes," *Origins* 41, no. 12: 194–195.
8. Witold Rybczynski, *Waiting for the Weekend* (New York: Viking, 1991).
9. Rybczynski.
10. U.S. Census Bureau, *Children's Living Arrangements and Characteristics*, Washington, DC: U.S. Dept. of Commerce, Economics and Statistics Administration, U.S. Census Bureau, 2002, http://purl.access.gpo.gov/GPO/LPS33039.
11. See MarriageSavers.org.
12. *Publishers Weekly,* December 30, 1996. Available at http://www.publishersweekly.com/978-0-393-04003-6.
13. Josh Levs and Monte Plott, "Boy, 8, One of 3 Killed in Bombings at Boston Marathon; Scores Wounded," *CNN*, April 18, 2013, http://www.cnn.com/2013/04/15/us/boston-marathon-explosions/index.html.
14. USCCB, *The Challenge of Peace: God's Promise and Our Response* (Melbourne: Dove, 1983), 147, 150, 159.
15. "Pope Repeats Plea for Peace in Syria, Lauds Relief Efforts," *Catholic World News*, June 05, 2013, http://www.catholicculture.org/news/headlines/index.cfm?storyid=18070.

16. John F. Kennedy, speech to U.N. General Assembly, September 25, 1961. Available at http://www.state.gov/p/io/potusunga/207241.htm.
17. Quoting *Familiaris Consortio,* 30, *Humanae Vitae,* 11, and *Humanae Vitae,*12; cf. Pius XI, encyclical, *Casti connubii.*
18. "Marriage and Family," *United States Conference of Catholic Bishops*, http://www.usccb.org/issues-and-action/marriage-and-family.
19. Cardinal Francis George, O.M.I., "The public discussion on 'same sex marriage'…" *Catholic New World*, June 9, 2013, http://www.catholicnewworld.com/cnwonline/2013/0609/cardinal.aspx.
20. Fulton J. Sheen, *Three to Get Married* (New York: Appleton-Century-Crofts, 1951).
21. E.F. Schumacher, *Small Is Beautiful; Economics As If People Mattered* (New York: Harper & Row, 1973).
22. Jeffrey Sachs, "March on Washington 50th Anniversary," *Huffington Post*, August 24, 2013, http://www.huffingtonpost.com/jeffrey-sachs/march-on-washington-50th_b_3810360.html.
23. Quoting *Sacrosanctum Concilium,* 122.24
24. Dorothy Day, "Poverty Is to Care and Not to Care," The Catholic Worker, April 1953. Available at http://www.catholicworker.org/dorothyday/daytext.cfm?TextID=647.